Lives of X

OTHER BOOKS BY JOHN CIARDI

Mid-Century American Poets, 1950
From Time to Time, 1951
Dante's *Inferno* (tr. and ed.), 1954
As If, 1955
I Marry You, 1958
Thirty-Nine Poems, 1959
How Does a Poem Mean?, 1960
In the Stoneworks, 1961
Dante's *Purgatorio* (tr. and ed.), 1961
In Fact, 1962
Dialogue with an Audience, 1963
Poetry: A Closer Look, 1963
Person to Person, 1964
This Strangest Everything, 1966
Dante's *Paradiso* (tr. and ed.), 1970

Books for Children

The Reason for the Pelican, 1959
Scrappy the Pup, 1960
I Met a Man, 1961
The Man Who Sang the Sillies, 1961
You Read to Me, I'll Read to You, 1962
The Wish Tree, 1962
John J. Plenty and Fiddler Dan, 1963
You Know Who, 1964
The King Who Saved Himself from Being Saved, 1965
*The Monster Den, or Look What Happened at My House and
   to It,* 1966
Alphabestiary, 1967
Someone Could Win a Polar Bear, 1970

Lives of X

JOHN CIARDI

RUTGERS UNIVERSITY PRESS

New Brunswick, New Jersey

Copyright © 1971 by Rutgers University, the State
University of New Jersey
Library of Congress Catalog Card Number: 76-125544
SBN: 8135-0668-9
Printed in the United States of America
by Quinn & Boden, Inc., Rahway, New Jersey

For Miller Williams
man, poet, brother

ACKNOWLEDGEMENTS

The first poem in this book, "The Evil Eye," is here reprinted from *From Time to Time*, Twayne Publishers, copyright 1951 by John Ciardi. The last poem, "Talking Myself to Sleep at One More Hilton," is reprinted from *This Strangest Everything*, Rutgers University Press, copyright 1966 by Rutgers, The State University. These poems are not properly part of the present sequence but are meant to serve something like the function of a frame around a canvas. It was Miller Williams who suggested I use them in this way and his suggestion, as usual, made sense. I am grateful to him for that and for much more. The margins of my worksheets are covered with his comments, gifts from the mind and talent of a loving friend. Of the poems within the main sequence, "The Benefits of an Education" was first published in the *New Orleans Review* when Miller Williams was its distinguished editor. "Cal Coolidge and the Co," was published in an earlier version in *Harper's Magazine*. Several of the others first appeared in the *Saturday Review*.

Contents

The Evil Eye

Nona poured oil on the water and saw the eye
   form on my birth. Zia beat me with bay
   fennel and barley to scourge the devil away.
I doubt I needed so much excuse to cry.

From Sister Maria Immaculata there came
   a crucifix, a vow of nine days' prayer,
   a scapular stitched with virgin's hair.
The eye glowed on the water all the same.

By Felicia, the midwife, I was hung with a tin
   fish stuffed with garlic and bread crumbs.
   Three holy waters washed the breast for my gums.
Still the eye glared, wide as original sin

on the deepest pools of women midnight-spoken
   to ward my clamoring soul from the clutch of hell,
   lest growing I be no comfort and dying swell
more than a grave with horror. Still unbroken

the eye glared through the roosts of all their clucking.
   "Jesu," cried Mother, "why is he deviled so?"
   "Baptism without delay," said Father Cosmo.
"This one is not for sprinkling but for ducking."

So in came meat and wine and the feast was on.
   I wore a palm frond in my lace, and sewn
   to my swaddling band a hoop and three beads of bone
for the Trinity. And they ducked me and called me John.

And ate the meat and drank the wine, and the eye
    closed on the water. All this fell between
    my first scream and first name in 1916,
the year of the war and the influenza, when I

was not yet ready for evil or my own name,
though I had one already and the other came.

Lives of X

Prologue: Letter to an Indolent Norn

Because they were crude and easy and without fixed
    expectation
  and could, therefore, accept what they got from me,
  interrupting permission only with lashes of temper
  I forgave in rhythm, lashing back
  word for word till the air was striped by our whips,
  and nothing else touched—I thank you, first,
  for the elders of the lost tribe I fell heirless heir to
  and left with no baggage but love, which is weightless,
  a first-day gift of rest in mother and father.

Seven days into the world, two miles from the picnic,
  his head leaking in traffic, his name a skid-mark,
  you broke the man from Sunday, maddened the woman
  all the eighth day jargon of her fears,
  then wasted her witless a long last linger of mush
  crying her veins itched, crying she was a bother,
  crying his lost name fifty years to must, crying
  the expense of nurses would sour me from her,
  then crying from habit, afraid, no longer of something.

And died, I can believe, in an instinct to spare me,
  on just the weekend I happened to be in town.
  From the funeral between two other appointments
  I flew home paid for, not even the travel wasted.
  Was his and hers my payment? "Ma, it's all right,"
  I told her at the last lid to nothing. "It was no bother."

Did you mean me to be glad? There at tribe's crone-cluck,
    whose telling leaked hanged sons like Hell shadow,
    I took you for true dark coming. Were you toying,
    those years you made me mad for God and guilt
    in sweats of prayer, then cut some thread
    and left me bored by my own agonizing? Did
    you cut it? or only break it one day beyond intention,
    yawning and stretching in the slowness of heaven?

For that, and for every chance you missed or made
        nothing of
    for whatever reason not to be taken for kindness,
    thank you. May all gods come to keep such
        slovenly ways.

Is mercy no more than the fed hawk's drowse?
    But I have been where you fed. I have felt wings,
    though never talons. What mercy
    is made of oversights? I was brushed and ignored.
    When I skidded the road was empty. When I fell
    nothing broke. What I loved stayed. It was always
    the next plane bloomed black, the next average.
    The bomb with my circle in it hit muck and burst
        buried.
    I was grounded by sniffles the day my crew went down.
    When the work party was strafed
    I was off stealing officers' whiskey, and got it.

I have these wing-tip memoirs, a freak numbering
    of chances too zany to bet on. Is that
    your game, and rigged? or are you, too, in it,
    and losing? However it goes,
    thank you. May you stay indifferent
    even to my wishing against you, and men
    win what they can and lose only at last what they must.

Then I think what games you *have* rigged. Is Harlem,
   for instance, your crooked casino? Was Dachau?
   Is India so pure a profit you have moved there?
   At your sub-headquarters in the black homosexual
   who claimed he contracted a habit while writing
     his book,
   the walls were clawed to bone-lath, the chairs
   were Spanish Maidens, the air was fishhooked full
   of a dust that cut lungs. He screamed toward the lucidity
   of an accomplished madness, and you
   broke his game with a coughing fit. He fell
   frothing and choking, his book a plaid of welts.

At tea in your rest home at the Happy Hilton
   the woman with the tattooed wrist came giggling
     in mink,
   played Lady Frolic through two drinks, then screamed.
   What ghost had you sent? Her husband cooed her,
     swaying.
   The house doctor needled her still.
   The room gaped oblivions the orchestra blared at,
   trying to drown in noise an alp of silence.

At your branch office in the Indian importer
   who spoke glass British chipped by American slang,
   the dice were pure tusk, ruby spots flush to bone.
   "The price of famine," he said, holding a lace.
   His terrible bargains he knew how to bargain
   needled the fingers that touched them. "Lovely,"
   the woman said. "Dirt cheap," he smiled.

Well, thank you for good enough in a bad market.
   I have suffered nothing I could not bear,
   pity and not be made to bear. I have watched losers
   look up from the last roll, stunned open,

plungers who came high-rolling and stayed to
    sweat down
to blood bets marked for broke: a road gang of lepers
who died a game ago or forever, begging bread
    to gamble,
blood to write home in, bone to cut spots on;
hags in Harold's alley whining to go down for five, two,
anything dice will roll over to stick men
stale on their bones, emptied out of their faces,
motioning, saying the words. In my fevers I hit;
grown cool, I played edges and nibbles, and won a little.
What sits by addicts and has no habit? Is an observer
a good enough thing? By the old wives of the tribe
at dark foretastes, I'll circle you wary: are these
your double-dealt odds?—to nag me easy
till I claw myself in the guilt of not hurting?
When the wino begs my dollar for the death he wants
and I give what costs me nothing, not even pity
for what I can no more help than he can, are
    you thinking
you'll hook me there? When children starve
    through news
and I send mercy the deductible check that will, likely,
make no difference, is that what you riddled,
to snare travelers, of the man who died immune?

It won't work. I guess you. I am not indifferent. Yours
    is the one mercy by indifference. Mine
    is given and taken. I expected less than I have come to
    and can give more than I meant.
                            Besides,
    I have died once, knew I would die, knew
    it would make no difference; but lived,
    and found I had been paid for. Lazarus rights:
    can all heaven imagine the ecstacy of first water

8

down the throat of the dead man risen? what it rinses?
what hymns in a sniff of moss? what practice
a dead man's love is? Somehow,
in a movie run backwards, a bomb implodes, soars
from the man's refitting and, in heaven again,
    starts over
and down in another sequence where being itself
is joy itself and sings for charred brothers
of the first film, too dirty to wish again.

Luck is an innocence: guiltless, I go free; or was guilty,
    met law enough, and need none now. I will bear
    what I must, ask nothing to bear, and may you
    sleep on the numbers till the numbers sleep.
    In your whim is our peace. May nothing prompt it
    from any indolence that will do for mercy.

The Shaft

At first light in the shadow, over the roach
like topaz on the sill, over the roofs,
the Old North Church spire took its time to heaven
where God took His to answer.
                          I took my drink
at clammy soapstone round a drain of stinks
and slid back into bed, my toes still curled
from the cold lick of linoleum. Ma was first,
shaking the dead stove up. Then Pa,
a rumble hocking phlegm. When the cups clattered
I could get up and climb him and beg *biscotti*
while Ma sipped cups of steam and scolded love.

The shaft went down four darks from light to light,
through smells that scurried, from the sky-lit top
where I built cities of kindling, to cobbly streets
that curved away as men go, round their corners,
to what they do after they kiss their sons.
Where *did* he go? He kissed me and went down,
a step at a time, his derby like a bob.
And then pulled under. And the day begun.

Later, when days were something that had names,
I went there with her, out of my sky-lit first
on the top landing, to the falling streets.

The stores were cellars and they smelled of cheese,
salami, and olive brine. Dark rows of crates,
stacked back to damp brick where the scurries were,
made tunnels in whose sides the one-eyed beans
were binned so deep I could lose all my arm
into their sliding buttons. In a while
I got my cookie and knew I had behaved.
Then up the shaft again, through its four darks
to the top landing where we lived in light.
A latched-on fence playpenned a world I made
of slant and falling towns. Until his derby
rose from the shaft and all the kitchen steamed.

God's cellar was one more dark. A tallow deep
where nickels clinked at racks of burning flowers.
Black shawls kneeled there whispering to the dead,
and left the prayer still burning when they rose.
He had such gold saints by Him in His dark:
why was God so dusty? Was He making
the dead from dust again because she prayed
and made me pray? Would all the dead be made
back to the shawls draped on those altar rails,
and come home singing up their shafts of dark?

I kissed the stone he changed to in his flowers.
But when he stayed away she would not waste
the prayers she lit but got him back in me.
His letters came. From God and Metropolitan.
A piecemeal every week. And he had bought us
half a house in Medford—out of the shaft
and into green that had a river through it.

And still he would not come back, the garden summer
nothing to him, the fruit with nothing to say.
My aunt and uncle bought the other half.

God had a house there, too, but would not speak
His first Italian to her. She came home
and spoke the rest to Pa, hissing all night
how much she was afraid. Or a dream rattled
and speared her to a scream, and the girls woke crying,
and ran to fetch her water, while I lay
guilty of happiness, half deep in books,
learning to guess how much hysteria
could be a style of acting, and how much
have its own twisted face, and how much more
could be the actress acting what she was,
panting and faint but gripping the glass of water
they always ran to fetch and watch her drink
till she sank back exhausted by medication
and let herself be fussed to sleep again,
satisfied as long as she was feared for.

So all was well. And if a glass of water
and the girls' fears were medicine enough,
why the girls would wake, the pipes would not run dry.

I lost her, and I lost them, shutting out
more night-rattling and more day-squalls
than I had sky for, there behind my books.
I made a cave of them and crept inside
and let the weather blow away unheard.

They had to run those weathers of the dark
forked day and night by lightnings of her nerves.
Not they, nor I, guessed half those howling years
the lightnings were her staff and they her sheep
to frighten close, all madness being fear.

And still they grew away because they grew.
And she came stalking after like a witch

when they strolled after supper. They found her out,
flitting from tree to tree with the black cat
of sniffed suspicion sliding at her feet,
a shadow in a shadow, and they led her
foot-blistering hikes through nowhere and back home,
slowing to let the shadow flit away
around the corner, slide into the house,
be dumped in a back closet, and not be there
to mar her innocence when she looked up
from sorting sorted socks at the kitchen table,
or sweeping the swept floor, and breathing hard,
but half believing their straight-faced innocence
as they clacked by to shut a bedroom door
on gales of whispering with giggly showers.

I read my book and guessed and didn't care.
An oaf in a madhouse. Keeping my escape
but staying on for meals. She learned at last
suspicion makes sore feet. But she wasn't finished.
Not while she still could faint and not come to
till everyone was crying in a circle
of guilt and glasses of water and grand opera.
I didn't know she was crazy. That we all were.

Nor that I dropped my book and lost my place.
I knew she had fainted and we were to blame.

Then, one night when the girls had invitations
her black cat hissed at, she stood in the doorway
ranting to turn them back, and when they argued,
she turned her eyes up, started breathing hard
and settled to the floor across the sill.
She had her act so polished by that time
she could sink like a dropped sheet, all one motion
and down without a thud. It was well done—

It took me in and sent me running for water—
but by whatever tells truth to the badgered,
it was too well done. When I came running back,
the girls had clucked her gently to one side,
pillowed her head, smoothed on a comforter,
and bent to kiss her cheek, cooing, "Poor Ma.
A nap will do her good." And off they clattered,
squeezing their giggles tight. Then even I—
the oaf of the litter—got it. I found the glass
still in my hand, started to put it down,
then drank it off. And, having watched that much,
sat down to watch the rest.
                               Were her eyes closed?
The girls' heels clicked across the porch and off it.
The last click jerked her upright in a rage,
but to one side, in case the girls looked back.
She hadn't seen me and I guessed she meant
to be found lying there when the girls came home.
God, what a weapon! I could *hear* her glower,
her lips grimacing vows to kill a saint.
"Have a good nap?" I said.
                               She snapped around,
head and body together in one shriek.
My skin crawled on a rasp of shame too late.
Then she was on me like her blackest cat,
its claws turned into fists. She beat so hard
it hurt me not to hurt. She'd hurt herself
unless I stopped her. Well, I'm an actor, too,
from a family of actors, I told myself,
and tried to clown it away. "Hey, Ma, lay off.
You'll hurt your wrist again. Come on, let's dance!"
The thing was to catch her mood and turn it around.
I picked her up—she weighed about ten pounds—
waltzed her across the room, her fists still going,
then settled her soft as dandelion fuzz on cushions.

"Just like your father, pig!" she tried to scold,
but her glower was out.
                              "So what? So it didn't work.
So now you can stop fainting. So what's lost?—
your stage career? It was a lousy act."

I'd kept my head just far enough above books
to guess my best chance was to play her husband.
"Just like your father," she scowled, but her grimace
quivered halfway to a smile. I thought I'd won.
But it slipped past a smile, turned into a giggle,
and out through a mad laughter to a scream
that had no actress in it but the fear
I was no husband to, and could not be.

—And gasped at last, since comedy is all,
to hiccups that went on until she lay
where comedy is nothing, strewn like lint
blown down into the bottom of a well
I could remember like the smell of tallow
inside a dark where racks of burning flowers
swallowed black shawls to altar rails of bone
down every turn and landing of the shaft.

If God still spoke her language there, I hope
she heard enough to promise her the light
I didn't know how to light her when I tried.

She did ease into age with half a smile
mending inside her. But her eighties raveled.
Her wits went back to muttering, and she sat
hugging a raggedy doll that would not light back
husband or son. And never saw us again
although we came and stood there in the shaft
bringing her pastries that oozed down her chin,

candies we had to wash out of her fist,
and jokes she did not hear the nurses laugh at.
She hugged her final dark to a rag God
who spoke in broken weathers to no wits.
And then we turned my father's grave and laid her
to take her time to Heaven in her last faint.

And there's a life, God knows, no soul would choose.
And if I send love after it, what's that
but one more scurry sounding down the shaft?

The River

By easy stations where time crossed and left
the banks ahead untouched, the river slipped
seven looped miles from springs to a salt mouth,
brackish a good five miles back from flood tide
but rock-fresh all its length into an ebb.

A cumulus of elm- and maple-green
was every summer, the heaven of it pierced
by a white-slatted Congregational spire
four-sided, with a clock for every wind.
And every wind and clock a story told.

A stone-fenced tidy Zion of thrift and God
the Congregational saints began there once,
their housefronts white on the hills yet, where I heard
the bells to Concord. In the clattering hour
history most chooses, midnight spurred its horse,
and Paul Revere came pounding at the doors
scarred by his knuckles yet—so I was told,
though only the pure-in-heart, the well invested,
and eagle scouts dead in the line of duty
can see the scars, not always.
                              Seen, unseen,
the saints rode west and northwest all one night
cross-country from green to green of the elm squares
leaving behind bad sculptures and good law,
enough to fill a countryside of causes.

Every nineteenth of April, though now by day
and with refreshments by the American Legion,
he rides again past children waving flags,
and beats on one door of one house still standing
as it was then, though it's a funeral parlor
these new days, though this day, the half day
it takes to fill the windows with DARs
in ribboned bonnets and tricorned gentlemen,
the corpse in residence must be wheeled away
and down the elevator to the cold room
till that year's rider clatters round the corner
where the horse van that dropped him at South and Main
waits at High and Winthrop to take him on
to the next house of the next town on his way,
already forgotten by the hoodlum young
storming the Armory for free ice cream
and bottles of what Boston still calls "tonic."

This is what I remember from a first.
A half day taken from the mailman's wake
to let a rider by, and a costumed clatter
over the dead man's interrupted state.
Locked in his cellar, he forecast forever
under whose stairs he would lie long the same
while hats and bonnets changed. That afternoon—
whichever year it was—I did my duty
beside his box in the light they brought him back to
before they wheeled him off again forever.

But first, a hoodlum with my hoodlum pack,
my flag and hand out, screaming with the rest,
I stormed the Armory for the Legion's handout.
And ducked out on him fast among his roses.
He was a good round chuckle every day

he hauled his bag, and every week he left
one more $10 piece of Pa in the slot,
and that was food and drink, and a quick Lord's Prayer
as Ma had ordered, and I could have the river
and he his promises.
                              The rafts and cockles
and leaky tubs I drifted summer through
touched every bank. Water rats quizzed my statue
at holes I knew. Dragonflies hummed me dry.
Alewives ran the flickering of their instinct
under my awe. I scooped them in their seizure
and sat seized in my shell, their slate-blue tremble
a mystery like quicksilver at my bare feet
in the constant inch of water beyond bailing.

Then, like the corpse put by for history's party,
or an undelivered mail, sender unknown,
they came one year and tasted their first water
and turned up the white mushrooms of their bellies
bloated like easy death and scummed with oil
in clots and rafts that stank back to the sea
and came up on the tide, and came and went
a week, ten days, till nothing came again
but a few eels too ugly not to live.

Is there a longer death than rivers die
out of the sainted valleys of their first,
following the mist-blown tribes and their dim totems,
and the congregation of saints beside the water
that came and went, and still came and still went
where black stumps of the rotted shipyards stubbed
the sewer-slimed edges of the rotted river?
Where, through the same green cumulus, the spire
the saints appointed as their arm to God

lifted its four clocks to the rose of winds
that took the captains out past God,

                          down river,
clearing Hull point, aslant to Provincetown,
and on to the Azores and Canaries.
Until the Trades grew wicked with their south,
the cargo was still God and Medford Rum,
with barter as it came.
                          But before landfall
on the Gold Coast, God's corpse went into the hold
and chain and shackles rigged them out as slavers
triangling to Jamaica in their stink
to trade what flesh had not gone to the sharks
for kegs of black molasses, and then home,
the hold scrubbed out with soda, God broken out
like a new flag to fly above the Square
where God's distillery waited for the syrup
to start a new firewater its three ways
from God, past God, to God again one Sunday.

Their portraits climb the stairs yet, or look down
from rows of deacons and from the bank's walls—
Nathaniels, Ebenezers, Jonathans.
Burnsided, muttonchopped, full-beavered, shaved,
bone-leathered, paunched, frill-collared, or homespun,
all crossed with a gold chain from which time hangs
to take out or put back as the trade turns.

Back to the Sundays when the sloops and barks
wove lines above the chimney tops, the wharves
silent, the gray dray horses out to pasture,
not hearing how the bells poured down from God
to call the Captain's carriage from the hill,
its two spang chestnuts, polished like new boots,
clopping between the pickets, and his Priscilla

bonneted prim but shawled in Indian silk—
a trophy from her trophy home to God
from mysteries of his untold own, but home,
a proper man and propertied and a deacon
with the white house still growing on the hill,
sprouting a new farm after every voyage.

God took them in. His minister at the door
came forward to honor him home, such blessings
He brings us once again from the main deep
to the good farms of the righteous. As one by one,
from offstage in themselves, squires with their ladies
passed, tipping their toppers, and God took them in
through the arched door, His portrait rayed above,
fingering the great gold chain from which time hangs.

And cleared his throat—a peal of organ sound—
when all but the tied horses swishing flies
had gone in from the Square and shut the door
on the concluded world with its beasts left over.

Sun in the morning. The river's grenades of light
blinding the ripples. Cock's matins sung. The crows'
black souls, like monks from a grimoire,
scudding back to their hills of warlock oaks.
A lamb bleating its last lawn before Easter—

When I left the river I could walk all day
inside one captain's name. The miles of farms
and tangled woodland his. Ebenezer Hutchens—
master at twenty, owner at twenty-four,
banker at twenty-seven. He died white
and dry as a peeled oak in his blind eighties,
whose bark and beard of youth had known the crows
from more hells than the congregation counted,

but owned the valley on both sides of the river
west of the Square and spire, and the crows' hills
north to the town line through the granite knobs
with black ponds, grubbed with leeches, in their shadows,
seeping to fern and deadfall where a day
blushed Indian pipes, white trillium, lady's-slippers
from bark- and moss-rot of cool bottoms,
the scrub untouched there from the first of saints
into that country.
                      Sun in the morning
to a pine-wood dusk over blueberry clearings,
I walked that one name, rounding its farms like ponds
in the wood shadow. At the Seven Hills,
its white cliff in the last light on the highest,
the Captain's House looked down on the toy spire
that was his boundary stake in the spread valley.
The ships were gone. The river dead. The wharf,
a coalyard drab with barges. The distillery,
blue-lawed to virtue once the trade had ended.
Molasses came from Boston.
                            A smoke from Sumter
signaled the Hutchenses, Bradfords, Woollseys
to the hot-running Gettysburgs of the righteous.
Even without trade, courage is a cause
and spills its blue boys long to the larks of God.

Old men of the GAR came out to march,
battle flags clearing the way for Paul Revere
every nineteenth of April. But on the hill
in 'forty-seven, Captain Ebenezer,
hunched at his desk of Honduran ironwood,
could tell a future. When abolitionist ladies
called in hymn-singing virtue to petition
against The Trade, and, thinking still as housewives,
complained that slave-ships stank—as if bad odor

were the offense of evil—Ebenezer
unhunched an instant, raised a Captain's head
out of his ruin and answered to first causes:
"Yes, ladies, slavers stink, but money don't."

And was dead himself before one son changed odor
under McClellan's nose, though well downwind
in the smallpox ghettos of the Potomac. Still
one son stormed Mobile and came home with contacts
that were no harm to trade. And another jingled
high Washington among desks that lost nothing
when money was to be made in the Sutlers' Peace.

The Armory took his name beside the river.
An outlet from its boilers steamed all winter
just at the waterline to let me dream
I knew a secret hot spring to the center
and walked on caverns hung with diamond darks.
While in the Armory's groins the Hutchens Light Guard
rattled the rifle range, shouted its numbers,
or changed to West Point uniforms on ball nights
and danced with lady-shadows past the windows
of the upper vault, my eyes glued to the light
that danced away and came and danced and came.

It was my country and a mystery sung
by bird, by brook, by squirrels chattering,
and shadows through the trees and old lies told
and histories tipping truths. The stone-farmed hills
hand-labored to their falling pasture walls
let fall a stone a season from their ruin.
The town was the invader. Dying barns
backed half the houses to a picket fence
and apple trees. Great bones of hand-chipped granite
trimmed off the squires' lawns, topped with iron fences.

Cellar walls three feet thick, with every block
of fieldstone a day's labor for two men,
bore oak-pegged beams, like ark work, or found money
building its city firm. But still the cows
roamed to the edge of pavement, and the weeds
poked through a cellar-hole that blotched half the Square,
where the first inn and first stage out from Boston
had rambled till its fire. And still the river
slipped easy as its first from the drowned boys
of summer at their play in sight of farms,
the clay pit, and the old wharf peppered black
where once molasses leaked a bait for flies
in the droning summer from the first, not long.

Then like a traffic's roar Boston spilled out,
first Irish, then Italian. A field at a time
the land went out. The Captain's house came down,
steam shovels ate his lawns, grazed his hills flat
for diagrams of two-by-fours drawn up
a day at a time and hammered shut, roofed, boarded,
given their doors, and left to find a name
with twenty years to pay at six per cent.
The Captain's bones flowered open to his grandsons
in vaults of promised paper with such names
as the valley had not spelled in all its time,
but still could add
                    payable to the order
of the Estate of Ebenezer Hutchens
a Bond and Mortgage covenanted with
Sean Flaherty and said estate to wit:
Aram Perunian and said estate to wit:
Carminantonio Ciardi and said estate
revised to Concetta Ciardi, widow, to wit:
that the lands and bounds and premises hereinafter
together with etc. heretofore

of the Estate of Ebenezer Hutchens
—pay off their life time or return to wit,
whose name, come off the land, returns to it.

A life. And better traded than for molasses.
My father traded his for four hundred weeks
of the $10 checks from Metropolitan.
Two mailmen died before his mail stopped coming.
I think my mother thought they were pallbearers
the government kept sending in his honor.
She liked wakes, and held one for every check
before she sputtered her slant name on the back
and wept it out for food. She knew some wrong
was being done her but was not sure which
and stayed suspicious on principle. Were we wronged?
our piece of a slaver's acre black with blood?
The tales I knew were old and wonderful.
Old and therefore wonderful. Old and dying.

And I was young and happier than her tears
could change me from. The filthy river slipped
smooth as its first. And all one prowling summer
when Will Howe got a job, I had day dibs
on his canoe, a leakless Indian legend
so tremblingly beyond my hammered sticks
that I could stroke the two miles to the Lakes
and prowl the pinefringe sure of mocassin tracks
under the bracken, or cut straight across
the mile-wide water further than the world,
unwronged by any day, in my own country,
whose dead I haunted and whose dead I am.

A Knothole in Spent Time

I have to believe it's a limited society
that remembers the Craddock School on Summer Street
where the tennis courts are now. Still, everyone
is local to his own ghosts. The one-room school
my wife rode spavined Josh to in Haw Creek
hid itself in a thicket for twenty years
after the school bus came, and then was sold
to Mr. Buster Robinson, who moved it
onto his place to house the hired man's family,
and let the thicket back over the well,
the two caved-in outhouses, the skip-rope yard,
the knocked-in stones no memory could sit long on,
though we strolled back for one that wasn't there.

A week before we were married we went down
and found the thicket onyx'd with blackberries,
went back again with a pail and picked it full,
ate them in cream so thick it wouldn't pour
but had to be spooned off the top of the pail.
Alas, the jewel thickets had been threaded
with poison ivy. Judith's arms went scaly.
She had to add long gloves to her wedding gown.
Then, when we took the Pullman to Chicago
the air conditioner quit and we lay sweltering
in a Black Hole of Calcutta. I caught a cold.
And all our honeymoon she scratched, I sniffled.
Our gem days in a sweet too thick to pour.

Are tennis courts a better end than thickets
that poison with their sweets? The elms came down
to let a pavement in. All change unghosts
something we change in leaving. Imagine Wordsworth
revisiting Yarrow—or Tennyson, Locksley Hall—
tourists to a nostalgia (why else go back?)
finding the place scrubbed out to Super Mkts,
cloverleaf ramps, and ten Drive-In Self-Service
Omnimats—they'd suffer a change of style
before they got the poem out of their dendrites
and into itself. I'm doing what they'd have done
at some last elmtop down from heaven's first
not for nostalgia but for nostalgia rebuffed.
My own, but a condition of us all
at the gates of lost infinities.
                              Craddock School
was hardly an infinity, but could spell one.
As anything begins. My mother took me
my first day gone into its creaking ark;
the huger, I have to guess, for my being small,
but huger again for all Ma's sermoning
on the sanctity and omniscience of school teachers,
as witness their salaries—almost as much as a cop's.
They were born in enormous palaces called "college"
and came to earth in kindness, that small boys
might "get an education" and "get ahead"
as nobody's parents had been able to,
which is why they were "sacrificing." At least why she was.

Which meant she'd strap me if I didn't behave.

Which meant, in the sad nonsense that speaks dearest,
she loved me and feared for me.
                              In I went.
It's out of focus now. I remember the elms,
a whispering sky that spattered sunlight through,

walls like the sides of a ship, and the ark roof
riding the elms in a sunlight of its own.
It must have been built soon after the Civil War
when lumber still grew on trees and was meant to be used
a tree to the ridge, a half tree to the joist.
It must have taken a forest for the studs.
Even on brightest days the hallway ceilings
were lost in their own dusk. It smelled of chalk,
the furnace room, and sneakers. It creaked and breathed
as if there were giants sleeping in its attics.
If heaven needed a barn for better beasts
than any of us were, the Craddock School
would have done for Apollo's cattle.
                                        I sat down,
pure in worship, ready to be saved,
and even to earn salvation. Miss Matron-Column
(I don't remember her name but she stood pillared
over our heads like a corseted caryatid
spilling out of her corsets on a scale
of two of anyone's mother) said what she said,
I don't remember what. I was having trouble.

Ma meant the day to be ritual, and had made me
a jumper-something called a Buster Brown,
and bought me new school shoes, and long white stockings
that buttoned, or tabbed, into my underwear.
I wasn't exactly comfortable but I took it
until a pug-nosed Irish snot behind me
—Tom something-or-other—got his needle in
to let me know white stockings were for girls
and that I was not only a Dago but a sissy.

I had set out to worship and be saved.
Now I'd have to fight when school was out.
The fight wouldn't be much, but it meant ripped buttons,

probably grass stains, maybe a red-lined nose,
and that meant Ma and the strap. I was better off
when I ran into trouble on troubled days.
But when the day began in a fuss of love
and then went sour, that meant I had betrayed her.
Which meant our opera played with the volume up
screaming to extra whacks with that damned strap.

While I was thinking that, I was looking around:
most of the girls, alas, had on white stockings
and none of the boys. The stinker saw me looking,
knew he had me, and began recruiting
more of the boys. Why did God have to waste
good schools on the lousy Irish?
                              —I heard a name.
"John Sea-YARD-i," Miss Matron-Column said,
"are you sure you are paying attention?"
                              I sat up
and tried to manage the look I guessed she wanted,
but I had forgotten even the stink behind me:
Omniscience had changed my name! I was John Sea-YARD-i
—and not even allowed to argue! What's a teacher
if she can't say a name right? . . . John Sea-YARD-i . . .
That was no sound of mine. I was John CHAR-di.
I knew that. And Ma knew it . . . well, what *did* Ma know?
House things, yes. And things about Italy.
But nothing about what went on out of the house,
such as how to say an American name in America.

I had been rechristened. All the way through high school
and my little while at Bates and my time at Tufts
—at both of which there were kids I'd started school with—
I was Sea-YARD-i. It took me seventeen years
and a bus ride out to Michigan—out past Canada—
to make my escape. And the first thing I did, free,

was to get rid forever of Matron-Column's
last ghost upon me and get my own ghost back
the way it sounded when its ghost began.

Meanwhile, to keep insanity in sequence,
we had our fight. I bloodied my jumper a fleck,
lost the buttons I expected to lose,
got grass stains on my knees. We tried our cuss words,
then backed off trading sneers and started home.

Ma would be waiting with that strap. My tail
would come away from it ridged. Then *she'd* cry,
and I would have to stop bawling to comfort *her*.
I've never thought far enough back—not for not trying—
to understand how we came to that arrangement.
I know it had something to do with my being ghosted
into her husband and he into her son.
Sometimes I think she was beating him for dying,
and me for not being enough of what she'd lost.

Something like fifty years later, when she'd faded
almost past touch and hearing in the Home,
but was still half remembering who we were
when we went to visit, and then forgetting again—
her long ghosts out, back in her ghosts again,
I sat beside her and she called me " 'Ndo."
(" 'Ndo" was her way of shortening "Antonio.")
What visitation in what mist was that?
Not he. Not I. A ghost halfway to black.
Then she drew back through mists I could not enter
even as a ghost.
                        Which year of what came first?
Time's all one once it's by. The ghost I walked in
was scheming its small way out of a ridged butt.
"Look what you did!" I yelled when I slammed in.

—If I could stake my claim as the offended
before she staked her own, I had a chance.
"These are GIRL stockings! I had to fight ALL the boys!"
(I never was stingy with flourishes. This was opera.)
"They called me a GIRL and tried to rip my stockings!"

I doubt it would have worked, all else being equal,
but my sister Edie came home just then from her school
full of hot news. "Ma, Johnny had a fight!"
she yelled, and waited around to see me get it.

Ma shut her up. "*Fati i cazzi tui!*"
—that's mountain barnyard Billingsgate, southern style,
for "mind your own phallic business." When Ma got earthy
she never was one to mind a little manure.
Except in recollection, those nine lives back,
I wouldn't even have noticed, except to know
I was off the hook once she shut Edie up.
"Take off the stockings," she sighed her martyrdom.
And when I had them off she tossed them to Edie.

"Somebody has to wear them," she said. "Go wash them.
—And you: get out of those clothes so I can fix them."

I changed to overalls and went back to the kitchen.
"Ma, the teacher said I was John Sea-YARD-i.
That's not our name."
                        "*Che nomi!* First your sisters—
now you. *Chi ne capisce?* Say what you like."
Then she caught herself: "You do what the teacher says."
I shrugged and started out. She called me back.
"I'm sorry about the stockings. I didn't know.
You want a *tarallo?*" (That's a hard shell bagel.)
"That's all right," I said. But I took the *tarallo*.

31

That did for my first day into omniscience.
I settled down to worship as I was told,
and wouldn't have thought not to. I learned to write
   "Squirrel"
with a bushy tail on the "q," "Look" with two eyes,
"Cat" with a whiskery "C"—proofs of a heaven
where things were locked forever in their names
as Nona and every Old Wife knew already
and could mumble charms for; as my Uncle Alec
could lay *tarrochi* pictures out of the deck
and read the next thing coming, that always turned out
to be something else, that on re-examination
turned out to be what the cards had really said
except that he'd read them wrong. The cards and teachers
(and, later, Mussolini) were always right.

I doubted the cards, and never took Mussolini
for heaven's hope, but of the omniscience of teachers
I was God-certified and rebaptized
in perfect faith—at least for one more year.
Then I found my first knothole in spent time.

I had been passed along from Miss Matron-Column,
Sea-YARD-i'd and still in awe, to Miss Absolute Void.
Don't take that name for disparagement: I was still
ready to play *cherubino* to all God's virgins
in our first age of innocence, but the fact is
I haven't a shred of her in my memory
except that she was the first chink in the wall
of heavens I had been schooled to as a faith,
though she didn't know it, and couldn't have been told.
I doubt she could have guessed the wall was there.

I droned fly-drowsy sun its leafy day
down through the elm's own daydream into mine.
The class was reading something, each in turn

rising to take a page—some Henny-Penny
or Puss in Boots. I'd read it twenty times,
and was off somewhere through elmtops in a float
when green clouds split to thunder. "John Sea-YARD-i,"
she called, her voice a judgment waiting to fall.
The book was on my desk but I'd lost the page.
I got to my feet. Somewhere in a separate haze
I remembered a girl reading and her last words
still floating in the elmtops. I held the book
and said from memory whatever Blind Mice
or Chicken-Little came next, pretending to read,
and knowing I'd make a slip, and read forever,
and DIDN'T make one! I must have been twelve years old,
having begun at six, before I heard,
"Very well, then. You may sit. And pay attention!"

I sat, relieved at first. Then burst inside:
I'd fooled her! She thought I had been reading! She was a
    Teacher
and *I* had fooled *her!* I started to tell the kid
ahead or behind or beside me or all at once.
Then hit on a truth as if I'd cracked my skull—
they wouldn't believe me! Ma wouldn't understand.
My sisters wouldn't care. Miss Absolute Void—
well, how could I tell her? I was alone
my first time into the world, at an edge of light
that dizzied like a dark; my gloat, half fear,
my eye at its first peephole into heavens
where Teachers were only people and could be wrong,
and all Ma's stations and candles could be rounded
by a truth I'd caught and held, and couldn't tell!

Thirty years later I did tell Merrill Moore,
though it was half a joke then. A slick squad
of thugs had cracked the Brink's Express in Boston
for the biggest haul in history, and over lunch

Merrill was theorizing they had to be caught
in spite of what seemed to be the perfect crime.

"Give them a year—or two—or three," he said.
"They're sitting on a world's record and can't claim it.
The money's cached: they wouldn't dare start spending.
Meanwhile they have to act as if nothing had happened.
Which is to say they're still bums among bums.
How long can a hero play at being a bum?
Some tart will give a man his walking papers,
a bar will shut off credit, a drunk will laugh.
Can a champion's ego hide in rags forever?
Ego's a king, and kings must claim their crowns."

"Maybe," I told him, "but what if you know to start with
no one will believe you while it still matters?"
And I told him how I'd found my hole in heaven
and seen Miss Absolute Void take off her wings
and soak her feet in a bucket of steaming water,
and never found a heaven whole again
nor anyone to tell about what I'd found.

"Well," Merrill said, "the Brink's Boys have the cash
to prove their story, wherever they have it hidden."

And so they had. I hadn't even the building
I could go back to and say, for whatever good
nostalgia of place might do me, "This is the room.
The first place in the world where I was alone
with more than I could tell of what was true.
Here something-nothing happened, and I remember
the day, the place, its ghost of elm-light falling,
and that I went through a door that wasn't there,
except that it once was real, and now it isn't."

And what is, but this lingering back of ghosts?

Feasts

My Uncle Alec's friend, Dominic Cataldo,
was straw boss of the treetop monkey gang
at Forest Hills, the woodpark cemetery
just at the edge of Boston. Across the street,
the North End's dead were tenemented tight
right to St. Michael's fence, stone crowding stone
and four names to a slab, but at Forest Hills,
down maple-dappled rhododendron drives,
the dead kept their suburbias lawned and sloped
to birdy hedges, brooklets, squirrel chatter,
and pheasant dells where dawn mist looked like snow.

St. Mike's looked like Pompeii on market day,
which must have looked like Prince Street excavated
after the stalls and pushcarts turned to stone
around the soot-streaked angels who froze there
in the act of reaching down to feel a melon
they never would pick up to bargain for.

The dead, like the Etruscans, kept their houses,
their neighborhoods, and their uses whole to God,
still zoned by ordinance. On Memorial Day,
a slope down from the villas of still money,
St. Mike's was at death's rush hour, the commuters
all carrying lunch and stiff wax wreaths to stone
past red-hot ice-cold hawkers. I planted pansies

I brought from home to border a last house,
prayed, ate my lunch, and spilled an orange tonic
that wet Pa's granite name, and prayed for that,
though it couldn't be a sin. I hadn't meant it.
I didn't even have another nickel
and had to drink tap water, iron-flavored.

Ma drank her tears awhile, then stilled to prayer,
then stood me by her in the receiving line,
her husband's name to her right, and sighed through
    neighbors,
cousins, *paesani*, and the delegation
from the Sons of Italy with its three-foot wreath
slant-ribboned *Presidente e fratello—*
Eterno in noi il santissimo ricordo.

It was her last of matronage, the one house
where she could stand, her husband at her side,
and welcome in the man's guests. All year long
she waited for that afternoon of graces,
once more a wife and ritual to his name
and presence. And all the loud hour on the El
and the half more on the trolley back to Medford
she sat carved straight to a found etiquette
she hadn't meant to lose, though late that night
I'd wake to hear her fear hiss through its dreams.

Still I passed Pa's grave more times than I stopped.
I spent more Sunday mornings at Forest Hills
than at St. Mike's. Which brings me to Cataldo,
to Uncle Alec, and to being bird dog
for the last organized gang of pheasant poachers
to operate within the city limits
of Boston, Mass; a gang led by Cataldo,
a long-armed, bow-legged, broken-toothed gorilla

with a chest of hair that coiled up like black smoke
from open collar to jawbone, and who was known
through all the bellowed treetops as Sputasangue,
which means "Spitblood," and was the heave-ho cry
he gave his sweaty gangs when backs were breaking
at crowbars and at peaveys and needed a lash
to break the boulder from the sucking till
or start the felled log over.
                                        I rang with joy
whenever Cataldo, halfway down his gallon,
turned into Sputasangue, the one artist
I ever knew to stretch a roaring curse
a full ten minutes and not run out of figures
nor use the same one twice. Religious poetry
lost a fountain the day he was kept from school
to weed his first dry ledge. The man could start
at the triune top and work the hagiography
down to St. Fish by strict anatomizings,
to frottery, battery, buggery, rape, plain mayhem,
and on to atrocious-assault-with-intent, compounded
twelve generations back and twenty forward.

He made me a bull-roarer once and showed me
how I could whirl the thing till the air shook—
Cataldo did. But Sunday nights in the kitchen
when Sputasangue smoked up from the jug,
I sat my corner and heard the vault of glory
split its stone arches and spin heaven and hell
in the avalanche of rhetoric, while Ma shook,
helpless in admiration, and Uncle Alec
bravoed the rhapsode at the root of man,
his flowering tongues.
                                Cataldo died of the shakes
a dry ghost later, but while he was a man,
the goatiest Greek down from the mountaintops

could not outhowl him on God's axletree,
nor chop it down so sighted to a line
that it would crack a walnut but not mash it.

Being half a Greek himself, he was a thief,
which is to say, a mountain fox. Forest Hills
was stocked with ring-neck pheasants that did so badly
in what seemed perfect cover, the hatcheries
had to ship crate on crate, month after month.
Something kept getting at them. Sputasangue
would go to the headman's office with a sack
of feathers, heads, and legs found in the bottoms
where skunks had left them, and would volunteer
to gun the varmints by the Trinity,
the twelve Apostles' crooks, and Lucifer's tail,
if he had to twist it off himself.
                                    That got him
the keys to iron gates. Sundays at dawn,
a throbbing touring car—a rusty Moon
that belonged to my Uncle Alec's friend Joe Pipe-dreams—
coughed through the gates. Uncle and Sputasangue
sat in the back, one shotgun left, one right.
Joe Pipe-dreams drove. I rode in front, cocked ready
whenever I got the signal, to jump out
and stuff the haul into a burlap sack.

Down in the dell, mist dreamed among the grasses
in the first light, and then a pheasant's head
would twitch up from no body like a snake
swimming but head high, half as Milton dreamed
Old Scaleskin for his cakewalk up to Eve
before God, Calvin, and William Jennings Bryan
condemned him to go crawling for the sins
he was already damned for in Tennessee
and the one-book farms of glory.
                                The old Moon

crawled at two miles an hour, Joe Pipe-dreams working
the spark and choke to make the thing backfire.
That flushed the birds. Then shotguns and backfiring
made one blur, till my uncle gave the word
and I went running with the burlap sack.

Our least haul was sixteen before the mist
drained to full day-ray. Later, Sputasangue
would walk his traps, finish a skunk or two,
and drop it behind the greenhouse for the headman.
Then he would empty the bird sack and twist off
heads, feet, and plucks of feathers in evidence.
He didn't have to be so foxy about it,
but man's the artist of his means. Art served,
we all drove back to Medford and gluttony.

Pipe-dreams and Sputasangue didn't want birds.
Not to take home. If they had a home, and I doubt it.
They played at hen-house fox as an act of nature.
Had the headman kept chickens, they'd as soon
have saved the shotgun shells. Why waste good money?
We didn't hunt: we harvested God's hand
and lived well out of it. As for those two,
they were both bachelors married to sour wine
they reeked of, and Uncle Alec, who made his own
(in the Aladdin's cave of barrels, bottles,
Mason jars, pickled peppers, crocks of lard
with half-fried liver balls layered in to keep,
apple chests drying under hanging herbs,
sausage, and drying grapes, the stacked squashes
by sand bins for potatoes, beets, and carrots,
under the footsteps sounding from the kitchen)
drew off a bottle of his best to start them,
and another when that went dry, and then another,
while Sputasangue made it up to rhetoric,
and Ma and Aunt Cristina, back from the fields

with dandelions and mushrooms, plucked the pheasants,
worked up the ovens to roasting, and started sauces
we gorged on for two hours in steams of heaven,
then slept off like a drunk, then woke again
to gorge again the last feast not to die.

Food was the flaming altar of the house.
All Hunger's tribesmen praise God as a feast,
fear him as famine, live as they can between.
Those birds were free grace and our week-long meat.
Hens cost money and were needed to lay,
and killing one cut into capital.
But free birds and free mushrooms sent a steam
up to the holy ghost that shines on harvests.

The stinking hen house and its morning bulbs,
green-smeared by droppings, was another bin.
Another was the garden where I sweated
my spring shame at manure I scooped from streets
and hauled home in a barrow while the fiends
who were my friends leered from the fence, and Riley,
the iceman, stopped his wagon to work me over
and offer me the next plop from his nag
if I would follow him.
                        But the Great Bin
was Albert's farm in Marlboro, twenty miles off
on pavement and ten in ruts, though that Joe Pipe-dreams
would have driven to Anchorage for the gas plus wine.

Every crop in, or when new mushrooms sprouted,
Albert would phone, and while Uncle Alec potted,
in or out of season, God's great day
of squirrels, rabbits, and anything with wings
(a robin in spaghetti sauce was a meat ball
that didn't have to be bought) I dug potatoes,

or filled my sacks with apples, pears, and corn,
while Ma and Aunt Cristina worked moss bottoms
of rotten trunks for mushrooms. We drove back
with sacks lashed to the fenders, milk cans rattling
the cheeses Ma would make late, Uncle Alec's
bloodstained knapsack tucked under my feet—
and that was food and faith and holiday
high mounded home in incense of oregano,
basil, parsley, bay, mint, tarragon,
and oils that crisped the body and the blood
of rabbit, squirrel, and of whole small birds
whose skulls we nut-cracked for the brain's sweetmeat
when every bone was picked. Then the house clinked
its dishes and the innocent sat glad,
leftovers shelving a next day's gift of grace
from open-handed heaven, whose clenched fist
had starved the mountain hamlets back to stone
deeper than Pompeii's, whose forgotten tongue
they twisted and still spoke for Heaven's
unanswering name; till sweating at their sacks
stuffed with the last of nothing, they went steerage
to heavens whose last gate was St. Michael's slum—
itself a heaven to which no man went starved.

I diet in suburbias past the dead
on checkbook lo-cal, or, a jet away,
pick at my sirloin among signing angels
who skip potatoes for a third martini.
Poor Alec's 94 and has religion
in both bad legs. He lives on the third floor
of what God left him, where he prays to God
to call him in before his legs give out.
I offered to pay the first-floor rent to spare him
those flights of stairs. He gummed a dunked *biscotto*
and shook his head too late a world away.

Those stairs were the one challenge time had left him.
His whined prayers were the tendons of his climb,
his diet of last dusts before the dead,
half dead already.
                              And still I had had my first
hound pup and shotgun from his living hand,
who lived beyond himself, locked forty years
in the shop under the El on Causeway Street,
but climbed his foxy Sundays to the feast
of God's permission to man's appetite,
and cheered on the bull-roarer in his power.

And were I God, and he back in My dust,
and I, in the infinity of My whim,
could give him back his prayers or appetites,
but not both—oh, as foxy as the foxes
I made of My own nature, I'd rig his answer
against the palsied maunder of his end
and send him back to Sunday in his power
over the gift-wrapped morning of the world
to its daylong feast and night-roar up from wine—
My man of plenty, ritual to his friends,
and honored home and hale, safe in the garden
that flowered forever, till it wasn't there.

Romancing with Our Beasts

Hot summer nights a space hum at my window
tweetered from grasses, woofered from gulping muds,
the signals throbbing up through one another
in some insomniac radio's reverie;
while from the Parkway just across the river
tires droned, shrilled, and hummed off, like a mosquito,
in three tones past my ear. How many sounds
is one sound? This hummed whistling while it whined
over the simmering wave lengths of the dark.

Outside the house, on this side of the river,
too heavily tuneless for their pitch to change
though they growled near, roared up, and growled away,
trucks from and to New Hampshire rattled South Street
till panes burred and beams muttered in their joints.
A quarter on the dresser rang awake
then droned back to the heaviness of time.

Across the river it was all pleasure traffic.
And in a hurry for pleasure, its tires ringing
speed-smooth macadam, a long shrill up and away
beside St. Joe's and through the Winthrop lights
wherever joyrides go, or drunks to bed,
or high-school kids to the moon. When the tires screamed
you could start to count, and if you got to ten
before the *krump,* no one was really hurt.

If it came by five, you'd hear glass crack its bells.
At less than five you could start counting corpses.

It took two minutes, including time for dressing
—half of it on the run—to sprint up South Street,
over the bridge, and across the river meadow
to where the beetle shells lay bashed and oozing,
or flipped dead on their backs with a last reflex
still twitching in them. Or over but still racing,
the wheels gone mad with no weight on their reason
and spinning up to a shrapnel of bad rubber,
sometimes a hail of bouncing meteors,
sometimes lashing a welt across the tank
to let the gas out, fluttering red and blue
like a one-winged butterfly or a Chinese fan
that wavered and collapsed and fell away
to let the dead beast die. If it didn't burn
and roar back higher than cop-lights to the moon.

So—except for burning—one topless monster,
its wheels past governance, lay on its back
flush to the road as if it were a barge
and the road its waterline. Firemen stood by,
brass nozzles aimed but waiting in case whatever
lay in the hold could still breathe. Till a wrecker
long-armed a bar that broke the gas connection,
then crouched astride the shell like a praying mantis
half lifting it, half tenderly, to its jaws,
while cops poked light beams into it, stopped, then signaled
to haul it over and open. And over it went.
Whatever dark it was the box of lit
for all to see—and there was nothing there
but the ghost of one white shoe in the outbound lane.

The wrecker hunched and panted. A red pumper
snorted, then eased its breathing. Cops waved by

the gaping traffic that pulled over and spilled
its tourists among tourists. At one corner
a black accordion sprawled across a drain,
gashed open, its strewn teeth swept back beneath it,
the player's corpse already blanketed
and shelved in the trembling ambulance, still ajar
for heaven and hell.
                        But can souls snatch their corpses
and take off without waiting? Where was this one?
The road was river meadow on one side,
and rotten woods, half swamp-sunk, on the other.
There was nothing on the grass. Cops beat the brush
where the fire truck sent a beam from its red lighthouse
to point the way to nothing in the mud suck.
For nothing. Till the beam slipped or was pointed
into a tree, and there above his hunters
the man lay scrawled, nailed open by a branch
that had to be sawed off to get him down.

What proof of what was I those wailing nights
up running from my sleep before it broke?
I never missed a death for being slow
nor a mangle for being timid. I was there;
the dark's first witness and the next day's news.
I needed every horror I could eat.
Or meant to have it, whatever it was I needed.
How do you keep a boy from being fast
to free disasters? I was the volunteer
at every carnage, the disgust of cops
—themselves thrilled with revulsion—who growled me off
but were always satisfied when they had cussed me
two steps back before I took three forward.
They swore that we are guilty of what we are,
and let me stay because I shared their guilt.
We were there in one emotion. Townsmen of it,

where every town has its own corner for it. Ours
was Winthrop and the Parkway—two intents
no traffic light could separate for long
while fools had wheels and nights had far to go.

And I had one more license: half the time
when I was up and running, I made it there
before the cops. There was an acoustic trick
built into the meadow and beamed across the river.
Somehow my window was an amplifier.
Or I was amplified inside myself
to tell by the counted scream, before it happened,
what was about to happen. When I grew older—
when I was home from school and had learned by blood
I needn't run for blood—I'd be on the phone
(we had one in by then) to the desk sergeant
before the echo thudded out. The station
was down the street on Main in a streetcar rumble
outside my echo chamber. In light traffic
a wreck could wait a life out still unfound.
But I could wail the cops there in shrill seconds
and be back to sleep before a ruptured tank
had washed the blood off in the public service.

Not that I ever asked to be death's puppy.
I woke nights being told and did what came,
sniffing revulsions till I'd had my fill
of how a body mangles, and could settle
for dialing mercy, such as it was, to come
and count the pieces, tending what it could.

The last bashed corpse I went to was Mike Flynn's,
and not across the river but wavering home
with God's own skinful picked up God knows where
and crossing South Street when some high-school kid

burned up from Main. I'd watched Mike times enough
come murdering two o'clock outside my window
due North by East-South-West in a looping lurch
from whiskey to a sot's end. He could weather
three yards to either side of a straight line
and three more luffing round to start again,
and call that walking home, and call his gargle
an Irish tenor, were he fit to call.

I heard him come, unreeling Mother Machree
out of a rusty gizzard, and—from nowhere—
one yelp of brakes, and instantly a bludgeon
whacking a bladder, and then the brakes cat-screeching
at least a ten-count after, and a tinkle
on the front porch and off.
                              I called the cops
before I even looked, then went outdoors,
turning the porch light on. A Model A,
one light still on, and up, its front wheels tilted,
was snagged on Kelly's hedge. On my own steps
I caught a glimmer of nothing that was mine
and picked up a smashed wristwatch with no works—
the case and an expansion band. (Weeks later,
while I was mowing, a blade snagged on a rust
that was a movement rotted out of keeping.
I held it like a chewed coin in my hand
and couldn't think what to think until I thought it
and flipped it into the trash can with dead time.)

Across the street cops were already flashing
where a Greek chorus of neighbors in grabbed wrappers
stage-whispered "Flynn! Mike Flynn!" above the mangle,
the breath still snoring in it, splints of bone
howling outside their flesh and, like a faith,
the reek of whiskey mounting higher than death.

He was so badly knotted on himself
it took a while to see one leg was missing.
Joey Damestri found it on a mallow
broad as a platter among the riverbank weeds,
and one of the cops wrapped the great leaf around it
to lift it toward what sacrament that was.

What ruin was the man? What ruin are we?
I saw, like those pneumatic tubes at Kresge's,
a dark from God's dark hand let this man down
exactly where he lay, his life inclosed
and blown to this one end; and we, like him,
blown there above it, exactly as we were,
choiceless as singing drunks their long dark home,
till we, too, are shed down a bank of weeds.

I gave a cop the watch case and its strap
just as I heard the breath snore up and stop.
Then thought I heard it again. But turned around
and it was the driver blubbering. "Look at him!
Oh, Jesus, look at him!" And then, like God,
or like a flight of His most jeweled angels
out for a fling and wailing as they dove,
the ambulance raved blinking down the dark,
gathered the jostled puzzle of the man
and, solved or not, took off with what it had,
and all was done.   And what was done? The boy
got two years for "vehicular homicide
with extenuation" or whatever it was
I half recall from legal idiom, meaning
reform school, but suspended and on probation.
For form's sake, I suppose. He *had* been speeding.
But Mike Flynn, if I knew him, had been swinging
from shadow to shadow. I'm not sure a bat

could have dodged him in his lurches.
                                        The neighbors and I
got nothing but a hair caught in our throats,
and the shriek of a sure knowledge that hissed down
to words again, and could be held and stacked
and spilled on grocery counters and pool tables
to prove we were authentic to that death
and had bent over it, gloating like men,
women, and children. Mad in our crouch of lust.
Changing to mercy when we could change back
to the faces we grow long in. But pulled short
those shuddering nights romancing with our beasts,
the rape we wait for in our stalest dark.

The Benefits of an Education:
Boston, 1931

A hulk, three masted once, three stubbed now,
carried away by any history, and dumped
in a mud ballast of low tide, heeled over
and a third swallowed in a black suck
south of the Nixie's Mate—itself going—
gave me a seal of memory for a wax
I wouldn't find for years yet: this was Boston.
Men with nothing to do plovered the sand-edge
with clam rakes that raked nothing. I walked home
over the drawbridge, skirting, on my right,
Charlestown ramshackled over Bunker Hill
and waiting for hopped-up kids to ride The Loop
and die in a tin rumple against the girders
of Sullivan Square, or dodge away toward Everett
and ditch the car; then walk home and be heroes
to ingrown boyos, poor as the streets they prowled.

There, house to house, the auctioneer's red flag
drooped its torn foreclosure to no buyer.
Now and then a blind man who could see,
and his squat wife who could stare out at nothing,
sat on the curb by the stacked furniture
and put the babies to sleep in dresser drawers
till charity came, or rain made pulp of all.
The rest lived in, guarding their limp red flags.
The bank was the new owner and that was all.

Why evict nothing much to make room for nothing?
Some sort of man is better than no man,
and might scrounge crates to keep the pipes from freezing
until the Water Co turned off the meter.
Or come Election, when men got their dole,
the bank might get the trickle of a rent
that wasn't there.
                    I'd walked those seven miles
from Medford to T Wharf to get my job
on the King Philip. Well, not quite a job,
but work, free passage, and a chance to scrounge
nickels and fish all summer till school opened
Miss Bates and Washington Irving.
                                    The King Philip
rose sheer, three river-boat-decks top heavy;
but she could ride an inner-harbor swell
and not quite capsize, though, God knows, she'd try.

Excursion fishing. She put out at nine
from the creaking stink of Sicilian fishing boats
praying for gasoline they sometimes got.
And came back in at five—in any weather
that might turn up a dollar-a-head half deck-load
doling four quarters into the first mate's hand
as if the fish they meant to eat were in it
and not still on a bottom out past luck.
Sometimes a hundred or more, but of them all
not twenty would turn up with a dollar bill.
It was all change. We called the first mate Jingles,
waiting for him to walk across the wharf
and spill his pockets into the tin box
in the Fish Mkt safe. When he came back
his name was Dixon and we could cast off.

Your dollar bought you eight hours on the water,
free lines, free bait, your catch, and—noon to one—
all the fish chowder you could eat.
                                        Good days,
the decks were slimed with pollock, cod, hake, haddock,
a flounder or two, and now and then a skate.
(A sharp man with a saw-toothed small tin can
can punch out Foolish Scallops from a skate's wing.
A Foolish Scallop is a scallop for fools
who eat it and don't know better.) I made a scraper
by screwing bottle caps to an oak paddle
and went my rounds, cleaning the catch for pennies,
or grabbing a gaff to help haul in the big ones.

Dixon, jingling again, took up a pool—
a dollar for the biggest cod or haddock,
a half for the largest fish of any kind.
No house cut but the little he could steal
and not be caught or, being caught, pass off
as an honest man's mistake in a ripped pocket.
The deal was winner-take-all. And the man that gaffed
the winning fish aboard was down for a tip.

One Sunday, with over a hundred in the pool,
I gaffed a skate we couldn't get aboard.
Dixon boathooked it dead still in the water,
then rigged a sling and tackle from rotten gear
and I went over the side and punched two holes
behind its head. Then we payed out the hooks
the fireman used for hauling cans of ashes
to dump them overboard, and I hooked it on,
and all hands hauled it clear to hang like a mat
from the main to the lower deck. We couldn't weigh it,
but it was no contest. Dixon paid on the spot.

He counted it out to fifty-seven dollars,
and I got two.
                    We took it in to the wharf
and let it hang—a flag—till the next day
when we cut it loose with half a ceremony,
mostly of flies, just as we cleared Deer Island.
The Captain didn't want that shadow floating
over his treasury of likely bottoms,
so we let the current have it.
                    After five,
the fireman rigged the hose, turned on the pressure,
and I washed down, flying the fish and fish guts
out of the scuppers in a rainbow spray
to a congregation of God-maddened gulls
screaming their witness over the stinking slip.
For leavings.
                    Fishermen are no keepers. One to eat,
a few to give away, and that's enough.
The scuppers might spill over, and the deck
on both sides of a walkway might be littered
with blue-backed and white-bellied gapers staring.

I cleaned the best to haul home. Or I did
when I had carfare, or thought I could climb the fence
into the El and ride free. Now and then,
Gillis, who ran a market next to ruin,
would buy a cod or haddock for nothing a pound
and throw in a pack of Camels.
                    And half the time
an old clutch of black shawl with a face inside it
and a nickel in its fist would flutter aboard
like something blown from a clothesline near a freight yard,
and squeeze a split accordion in her lungs
to wheeze for a bit of "any old fish left over,"

flashing her nickel like a badge, and singing
widowed beatitudes when I picked a good one
and wrapped it in newspaper and passed it over
and refused her ritual nickel the third time.

"I can afford to pay, son."
                              "Sure you can."
"Here, now, it's honest money."
                                    "Sure it is."
"Well, take it then."
                        "Compliments of the house."
"God bless you and your proud mother,"
she'd end, and take the wind back to her line.
Then the Fish Mkt man got after Dixon
for letting me steal his customers. Nickels are nickels:
for all he knew, I might be stealing from him
out of that pocket of nothing. But I foxed him.
Next time the old shawl came I sent her off
to wait by Atlantic Avenue. (And I'm damned
if the Fish Mkt man didn't call to her
waving a flipper of old bloat, calling "Cheap!
Just right for a pot of chowder!") After that,
I made an extra bundle every night,
cleaned and filet'd, and when she wasn't there
I fed the cats, or anything else of God's
that didn't run a market.
                              Then five nights running
she didn't come. Which, in God's proper market
might be more mercy than all nickels are,
whoever keeps the register, whoever
folds old shawls for burial.

                              Some nights—
once, twice a week, or some weeks not, the ship
was chartered for a stag by the VFW,

54

(we used to call them the Victims of Foreign Whores)
or some lodge, or some club, though the promoter
was always the same stink in tired tout's tweed.
He rigged a rigged wheel forward on the lower deck.
Sold bootleg by the men's room. Used the Ladies'
as an undressing room for the girlie show
that squeezed its naked pinched companionway
to the main deck "salon" to do the split
or sun itself in leers, clutching a stanchion,
or, when the hat was passed, to mount the table
and play house, if not home, two at a time,
with a gorilla stinking of pomade
who came on in a bathrobe from the Ladies'.
Two shows a night, prompt as mind's death could make them
while it still had a body. And on the top deck,
for an extra quarter, Tillie the Artist's Model
undid her flickering all on a canvas screen
lashed to the back of the wheelhouse, where the Captain
kept a sharp Yankee watch for the Harbor Cruiser.

He was a good gray stick of salt, hull down
in some lost boyhood that had put to sea
with the last whales still running into myth.
And down to this, or be beached flat, keeled over
like Boston, or that hulk off the Nixie's Mate,
to stink in the mud for nothing.
                                    Nevertheless,
It was some education in some school.
I panted at those desks of flesh flung open,
did mountains of dream homework with willing Tillie,
and, mornings, ran a cloth and a feather duster
(God knows where it came from—I'd guess Mrs. Madden
who cooked the daily chowder of leftovers
in her throbbing galley) over the counters, chairs,
and the great ark-built table, still flesh-haunted.

If it wasn't an education, it was lessons
in something I had to know before I could learn
what I was learning. Whatever there was to learn
in the stinking slips and cat-and-rat wet alleys
off the black girders and the slatted shadow
of the Atlantic Avenue El in Boston
where the edge-grinding wheels of nothing screeched
something from Hell at every sooty bend
of the oil-grimed and horse-dolloped cobbles
from Federal Street to the West End's garlic ghetto,
where black-toothed whores asked sailors for a buck
but took them for a quarter, in the freight yards,
or on the loading platforms behind North Station,
or in any alley where the kids had stoned
the street lights to permission.
                                        I took home
more than I brought with me of all Miss Blake
and Washington Irving knew of Sleepy Hollow.
(It had stayed clean and leafy I discovered
years later—like the Captain's boyhood
waiting its fo'c'sle south of Marblehead—
yet, a day further on the same road West,
the hollows had turned grimy, and the hills
fell through tipped crowns of slag—like Beacon Hill
stumbling through trash-can alleys to Scollay Square.)

Still, I got one thing from my education.
One stag-night when the tired tout's bootleg sold
too well for what it was, four poisoned drunks
lay writhing in the stern on the lower deck
in their own spew. And one, half dead but groaning,
green in his sweat, lay choking and dry-heaving,
his pump broken. While from the deck above
girls clattered, the pimp spieled, and the crowd raved.

Dixon came after me with the tout. "Hey, kid,
got a good stomach?" Dixon said. "Yeah, sure,"
I told him, honored.
            "It's a dirty job."
"What isn't?"
            "Five bucks!" said the tout. "Five bucks!
Here, Johnny. Five bucks cash and you can hold it!
My God, the guy could *die!*"—and passed the five
to Dixon who spread it open with both hands
to let me see it before he put it away.
"And a deuce from me if you'll do it," he tacked on,
taking my greedy silence for resistance.

"Who do I kill?" I said, taking the line
from George Raft, probably.
            "Look, kid, it's legal.
You *save* a guy!" the tout said in a spout.

"Lay off," said Dixon, and putting his hand on my shoulder,
he walked me off two paces. "It's like this.
The guy's choked full of rotgut and can't heave it.
I tried to stick my fingers down his throat
to get him started, but I just can't make it.
Kid," he said, "it takes guts I ain't got.
You got the guts to try?"
            And there I was
with a chance to have more guts than a first mate,
and seven dollars to boot!
            "Which guy?" I said—
only for something to say: I knew already.

"The groaner by the winch. I got a fid
to jam between his teeth if you'll reach in
and stick your fingers down his throat."
            We raised him,
half sitting, with his head back on the chains,

57

and Dixon got the thick end of the fid
jammed into his teeth on one side. "LET'S GO, KID!"
he screamed, almost as green as the half-corpse
that had begun to tremble like a fish
thrown on the deck, not dead yet, though too dead
to buck again.
                    But when I touched the slime
that might have been his tongue, I couldn't make it.
"Dixon, I can't do it!"
                         "Well, damn your eyes,
you *said* you would. Now put up, or by God
I'll heave you over!"
                         "Wait a minute," I said,
catching my education by the tail.
"Can you hold him there a minute?"
                                   "*If he lives.*
Now where the Hell you going?"
                               "I'll be right back,"
I called, already going, "I'll be right back."

I ran for the locker, grabbed the feather duster,
and ran back, snatching out the grimiest feather,
took out my knife, peeled off all but the tip,
then fished his throat with it, twirling the stem
till I felt him knotting up. "Evoe!" I shouted
for Bacchus to remember I remembered,
not knowing till later that I mispronounced it.
"EE-VO," not giving Bacchus all his syllables.

"Heave-ho it is!" roared Dixon and ducked aside
as the corpse spouted. "There, by God, she blows!"
And blow she did. I've never seen a man
that dirty and still alive. Except maybe the tout
clapping me on the shoulder. "You did it, kid!
By God, you did it! Johnny, didn't he do it!"

Dixon wiped his hands on the drunk's back
where he had twisted and sprawled over the winch-drum
(what reflex is it turns a dead man over
to let him retch facedown?) and fished the five
out of his pocket. "Where'd you learn that trick?"
he said as I took the money and waited for more.

I could have told him, "Dmitri Merezhkovsky,
Julian the Apostate," but it wasn't
on Miss Blake's list, and certainly not on his.
"How about the other deuce?" I said instead.

He was holding the feather duster by the handle
and turning his wrist to inspect it from all sides
and looking down into its head of fuzz.
"What's this thing doing on a ship?" he said.

"Waiting for Romans," I told him, guessing his game
but hoping to play him off. "That's history, Dixon.
When a man went to a banquet and stuffed himself,
he'd head for a men's room called a *vomitorium*,
tickle his throat with a feather, do an upchuck,
and then start over. How about that deuce?"

"If you're so smart, then you can figure out
I said if you used your fingers."
                              "Hey," said the tout,
"If you ain't paying up, get back my fin!
If you can welch on this punk kid, then I can!"

"Go peddle your sewer sweat," Dixon said. "Here, kid.
You earned it right enough. Go buy yourself
more education." And stuffed into my pocket
a crumple I unfolded into—one bill,
while he went forward, shoving the tout away.

Six dollars, then. One short. But the first cash
my education ever paid, and that
from off the reading list, though of the Empire,
if not the Kingdom.
                    Meanwhile, the hat passed,
the crowd's roar signalling, the pomade gorilla
came from the Ladies' and pushed up the stairs
from his own *vomitorium* to the orgy
where low sisters of *meretricis honestae*
waited to mount their table through lit smoke
into my nose-to-the-window education
one deck below the Captain's Yankee eye
on watch for the Harbor Cruiser and the tide,
bearing off Thompson Island to the left,
Deer Island to the right, and dead ahead
Boston's night-glow spindled like two mists:
one on the floodlit needle of Bunker Hill,
one on the Custom House, both shimmering out
to sit the waters of Babylon off Boston,
whose dented cup—an original Paul Revere
fallen from hand to hand—I drained like the kings
of fornication, mad for dirty wine.
And for the kingdoms opening like a book.

Cal Coolidge and the Co
(Poem for $98.41 plus, hopefully, bonuses.)

Monday's child in Boston looked like soot
on blackloaf cobbles under the screeching El
on Causeway St. Friday's child looked like fishguts.
Through all the rat-faced week I ever saw
fouling its gutters, Judson Treadlowe Marshall
looked like Calvin Coolidge. Or like a man
who looked like Coolidge looking in a glass
to wonder how he had missed being President.

That's two resemblances, or one and a half,
plus fishguts, soot, and all the mudflat week
in Boston Mass for the saint-misted names
and the frame around them. Add a high stiff collar,
a pin-knot head bookkeeper's tie, a jawbone
bulging with its grip on integrity,
and what you have will do for J. T. Marshall
doing for Calvin Coolidge at about
eleven cents on the dollar
                          —against which I,
hereby, as of this date I sit to write,
being June 30th, 1966,
lay claim to ninety-eight dollars and forty-one cents.
Meaning I'll take more but won't settle for less.
And I've waited long enough. This is the story:

Getting a job in 1933
was family grapevine business. What jobs there were
were hanging out no shingles. You found your door
when someone you knew knew someone.
I was just out of high school with nothing to do
and less than half a start toward college money.
I needed a paycheck anywhere there was one.
After a while John Follo, my *compadre*,
made the connection.
                              John Follo was a barber.
He and my Uncle Alec and Frank Fiore
made half of nothing a week in a ratty shop
under the El, a block south of North Station
and cater-corner from the Biscuit Co.

J. T. Marshall—*Meestra Maresciallo*—
was head clerk at the Co, and what they had
for gentry in the shop. When he walked in
even Frank Fiore stopped bellowing Mussolini
and *Italia irredenta*. Any customer
was one more quarter and maybe a nickel tip
—which was pedigree enough on Causeway St.—
but *Maresciallo* was a *gentilaman*—
a daily shave, a haircut once a week,
 nd one of the Lords of Life who Hired and Fired.

I used to shine his shoes when I was a kid
squeezing for nickels, but my *compadre* John,
who liked a gesture, never would let him pay me.
And J. T. Marshall, who seemed to like his nickels,
never insisted hard enough to lose one.
Not that I lost out by it—my *compadre*
was not a man to charge me for his gestures.
He always paid for God once God had left.
—But I could still think what I wasn't saying

because the *compadre* would rather it wasn't said.

Who knows what pious drivel and kowtowing
John Follo—rest the sweet soul of a man—
sang and danced to, talking me up to a job
over hot towels, Bay Rum, and Lucky Tiger.
I know I came out of it at least a saint
for J. T. God said yes and I was called
by His elected messenger, my *compadre*,
who took two hours to lecture me half enough
on the divinity of J. T. Marshall
and on the deference due him.
                                    Fair enough.
He needed deference. I needed a job.
I'd trade him need for need.
                                    On the Chosen Day
I walked in like a choirboy and sat stiff
as Yessir, Nosir, and Fifty Merit Badges—
thirty-seven of which I did once have
in the first sewing on of an ambition.
Badged, unbadged, but scrubbed to halos, I sat
while J. T. read the Sermon on the Biscuit
from Ambition through Integrity to Zeal.
There, while the El trains screamed by unavailing
outside his window and his mottoed wall,
he let me know the future lay ahead.
And though the present started at the bottom,
who knew but what in forty faithful years
I might not sit—well, not at *his* high desk,
but maybe on the same floor, in a corner,
where every day while I was being true
I, too, might keep a motto to its wall.

—And down to business. I got the job.
Shipping room. Night shift. Punch the clock by eight,

work till the trucks were loaded. The good Co,
whose name and prayer were service, guaranteed
next-day delivery. While the shipping crews
wheeled up their carts, Gallagher at the gate
chanted his night-long litany of Kute Kookies
to the crew's antiphon, and three of us
illuminated triplicate manuscripts
of Honey Hunks, Goo Globules, Marshy Mounds
with marginalia of price and poundage
row after row, cross-checking, pulling carbons,
piddling progress through its long subtotals
to its grand nothing at fourteen bucks a week.

And glad to have it. I'd have done more for less.
Though not in virtue's name. Or not as virtue
came memoed down the tube from J. T. Marshall;
concerning which and whom, John Follo told me
my third day on the job, I was to pay him
for a Stetson he had bought for J. T. Marshall
who was too noble to pocket my first week's pay
as his employment fee, but who had chosen—
with some reluctance, I was made to know—
a pearl-gray prize at Hymen's Haberdashers
for which John Follo had paid, for which I owed him
twelve dollars and ninety cents. Well, I had paid
for every cockroach job I ever got.
This time I even saved a dollar-ten.
Such was my dividend from the higher ethics
of Judson Treadlowe Marshall. And four months later
a raise to sixteen dollars.
                              I was rich:
a dollar a week for carfare, one to spend,
and twelve to bank—at first—and then fourteen.
J. T. could have had Sears Roebuck's best tin halo
if they'd had one to fit him, and welcome to it.

But never doubt I meant to get mine back
in hard cash—and with interest—for hard cash.
Not that I held a grudge. A Stetson delivered
to Old Integrity as the price of the faith
is nothing to hide a bilious night-light under
for thirty-three years. And J. T. God drained dead
into his own glass inkwell years ago.
I wouldn't hold a grudge against a ghost,
not even one that looked like Calvin Coolidge
snitching fedoras and shoeshines from the poor.
It's just that I'd sooner turn a fool to advantage
than lose my advantage of him.

                      Besides, I promised.
Promised myself, that is.

                    One August morning
of 'thirty-four (I had been accepted at Bates,
had cash enough to eke out the first year,
and had given notice) I was called upstairs
by Calvin J. T. Coolmarsh.

                He had his desk
(as I might have said before, but now will do)
at one end of the aisle, like half an altar
(the lower half) whose glory managed yet
to shine down on the stalls of bent gray saints
at ghostly homage in their Curia.
The wall said: THINK. And: YOU ARE YOUR OWN FUTURE.
And, in four colors: NEW! KASHEW KA-RUNCHIES!

Against the wall, lighting these sacraments,
a hat rack rose resplendent to the Lord
in oak of the True Cross. Upon it shone,
straight to my soul as I sat facing Him,
the Pearlgray Perfect Stetson of Great Price,
its purity undimmed by the dark year.

"College!" the High Priest said. "Well, now. Well, well, now!"
(He liked a round beginning twice around.)
"We like to see a young man get ahead."
(*And old heads get new Stetsons*, the oak whispered,
dancing a little as a train shot by
just at the window, strewing splinters of light.)
"Still, if I'd known you hadn't meant to stay . . .
you know we think of ourselves as a family. . . .
I don't know what we'll do for a replacement. . . ."
(*Spit out the window*, I thought of telling him.
*Lift the first hat you hit. If what's under it
can hold a pencil and can see the sidewalk,
that's twice enough for any job you've got.*)
". . . A question of loyalty and clear understanding,
you understand. . . ."
                    I said I understood.
I said I was grateful for the opportunity.
I said my heart would ever be with the Co
and the family of Cal Marshedge and J. T. Coolshell.
He said he would shake my hand and wish me luck.
The hat tree shook again. The Stetson's ghost
called from my *compadre*, "Remember me!"
He said, "Good-bye." I said, "Good-bye, sir. Thank you."
He said, "Be worthy of your opportunity."
—What could I say to that? It choked me up
to think what sentiment was in that man.

I stumbled out the door and into the Waldorf
(the cafeteria, not the hotel).
There, over coffee-and, I sat and wrote
"12.90" and then figured 6%
compounded annually for fifty years
from 1933, and drew a circle
around the last date, 1983,
and wrote "to be collected before then."

And swore it by the oak of the True Hat Rack
until it flower again at the last Easter,
or till the last fool's dead in Boston, Mass,
or till it's eight P.M. at the Biscuit Co
on the eve of the Last Delivery, or until
I had turned one damnfool to my advantage
or lost my advantage of him and gone damned
for being more fool than what I call a fool.
And damned if I'll be so damned.

                    That's why this poem,
whatever it lacks of merit, won't lack point
if I can sell it to some fool editor
for a minimum of $12.90 at 6%
compounded, as of 1966,
for thirty-three years—which comes out, as I have it
(I don't remember what I figured then
but I called my insurance agent, and take his figure)
to exactly ninety-eight dollars and forty-one cents,
claimed from and for the ghost of J. T. Marshall,
along with such bonuses as may be due me
for having studied the arts of exorcism
(which only a fool, let me insist, will sneer at).

Postscript

In '68—as I want a ghost to know—
I sold this poem to *Harper's* for two hundred
and fifty dollars. That's cost plus bonuses
plus satisfaction. Jack Fischer wrote to say
it was the most *Harper's* had ever paid
for a single poem. I take that as one more bonus,
and as proof there is a market for exorcism.

I could have bought it myself to run in SR,
which would have paid at least five hundred for it,
but it wouldn't have been the same. I wanted the money,
but I wanted someone else to say I had earned it.
How else could I have proven to a ghost
I hadn't been lying to it half a lifetime?

I've marked it Q.E.D., and banked the check,
and awarded myself the Oxford Dictionary
(at 25% off three hundred, list)
and took my wife to lunch at The Four Seasons.
That left me four dollars down, with taxes to pay,
but the books are deductible as office equipment,
and my wife is business, being subject matter,
which makes her deductible on a blurred receipt.
I'm afraid that brackets her with J. T. Marshall,
but I'm closing *him* out (so I shall insist
if the Revenuers insist) as a capital gain—
and that's a difference not even he would argue.

That's the account sheet. Someone is always asking
how poets make a living and no poet
has ever written to say. Some years back *Playboy*
asked me to write a piece on just that subject
and offered me fifteen hundred for it. I told them
I tried to live as a poet but made my living
by shrewdness, and had been shrewd enough—with luck
(which means I guessed well on a rising market)—
not to need fifteen hundred. Say it would take
a week of a wrong attention to write that piece:
it comes out as no bargain.
                                    I've grown pure
in having all I need this side of greed,
and I have more congenial sins to work on.
A man is what he does with his attention

and mine is not for sale, though I'll take cash—
and gladly—for whatever my attention
turns to for its own sake, when I'm finished with it.

Let this be my leave offering to the ghost
of J. T. Marshall, and of twenty others
who bought me cheap, and couldn't afford me now,
because I can't afford to be afforded
by anyone but myself, or I'd lose the ghost
of how I live, however I make my living.

And so to my last bonus, which is the first.
Any man can learn to learn from the wise
once he can find them; but learn to learn from a fool
and all the world's your faculty. I leave here
one ghost lighter but, finally, with a thanks
to the ghost of J. T. Marshall, emeritus,
who left his hat on an unmysterious tree,
but taught me what he didn't know himself.

A Five-Year Step

I don't remember what I was arguing
in H. H. Blanchard's Medieval Lit.
at Tufts in '37—something to do
with numerology, and I knew about it
the way my cousins knew baseball statistics
by having been raised inside them, but couldn't prove it.
"It does sound plausible," said H.H.B.,
"but how do you know if you can't document it?
Remember, we're not discussing how *we* feel
but what went on in the mind of the Middle Ages."

"That's just the point," I told him. "I was born there.
Or else I was born beforehand to where they came."

And if it was half a flourish for sweet style's sake—
not for a class of dolts to titter at
though they had to have their titter, and let them have it—
it still was half as true as I was born.
Maybe half as true as anyone is born,
and with no proven Renaissance to follow.
At least I haven't met Lorenzo's ghost
in any court I've come to, nor Leonardo
at the Academy, nor myself afire
with dawn enough to strike spires from the day.

Sometimes I think I've made it out of the dark
but not into the light. There may be light.

But what's in the Control Rooms is a glow
dim red as altar tapers, and as faithful
to the Holy Ghosts of needles on their dials
trembling with Presences.
                            As I was born—
to dim red glows I sensed but could not read
except to know there are Presences, and to learn
the first of everything is a lunacy
whose chatter starts before us in the dark.

A cave of colored windows where God's light
came down in shafts bored through His core of stone
closed me in good and evil, and I was wrong,
my natures all veined sinful before starting.
I felt His eye bore and His great grab reach
to sulfurous ores soul-deep in half my dreams.

And from the rails and galleries of that dark
and at its pitheads, black-flagged orators
of tongues that were never mine sermoned me through
to guilt and the Irish Trinity. Ma wept
to hear how God denied His round Italian
for a nose full of South Boston Jeremiads.
Nights, I could hear her arguing with Pa
to take the matter up with San Michele
or with San Giovanni of his own son's name.
But we couldn't be sure he had made it up that high.
Weren't we still praying him out of Purgatory?
However it was, we never got an answer.

I did what was done to me and fell asleep
falling off roofs and clouds to wake up screaming,
holding my genitals that had fallen off
because they belonged to the Devil and he'd come for them
and changed me into a girl for punishment.

But in another sleep I was all escapes.
I killed Cavalcante who had killed my father—
he shouldn't have driven so fast—and ran back home
and Pa himself was there and gave me wine
in three red glasses, because I was his son.
Himself the tall first number of the bottle
he filled me from. And Ma, an eight, behind him
in the two great circles he had married one.

I didn't know then my dreams were from a mountain
where every town defended its own Virgin
just as the Greeks had left her in a cave.
But I could tell St. Patrick was none of mine,
though at St. Joe's his feast day waved more flags
than God broke out for Easter and Christmas together.

What was I then? Thirteen. Maybe fourteen.
Like Ma, I half believed I was safe in God
and what God we were safe in. I couldn't have guessed
we were Greeks who spoke ourselves in bad Italian
from a parish of goat thickets, civil war,
and hot blood on the mountain—all our saints
disguised as Catholic but as mountain-rank
as a day's sweat on the ledges of the starved
who put their prayers into thickets. I had left
St. Joe's before I left and didn't know it.
It took a clown to rip my thicket loose:
and in came Father Ryan blowing his nose
one warm March day to lather the Sunday School
in his own idea of a hagiological rally
for the Big Green Team. And sent the mountain sliding
down on the cave forever.
                                        His nose well blown,
he stood above us, outside the altar rail
and worked the boys up to three last Green Cheers:

"Where did St. Patrick come from?"

                              "Ireland!" the saved screamed.
"And where did he bring his blessing?"

                                        Again: "Ireland!"
"And where did your fathers come from?"

                                        Once again
he got his chorus but he lost my soul.
I heard a bellowing of lunatic treason:
"FROM ITALY, BY GOD!"

                              And didn't know
I was the lunatic till he grabbed my ear
and dragged me to the altar: "PRAY FOR YOUR SOUL!"

But I'd be damned first. I stamped out of there running
the wronged rage of the blind who have no world
or would sooner knock it over than be trapped.
Later, he said I stamped my heel on his instep.
I won't deny it. He did limp for two weeks.
And world as it was, though I was innocent
by memory and intention, I'd used that trick
a time or two to make a fool let go.

I'd had my skull cracked once for being slow.
And Toots Fitzgerald still has a bad shoulder
from learning I learn fast. He ran me down
with obvious intent to teach me something
I wasn't inclined to learn. He was fifteen
and I was a snotty ten the day of our lesson.
Though as it happened, I ended up teaching him
what I hadn't learned myself before I did it.

I took off down the middle of Summer Street
but with too little start. Toots pounded after
five good years faster, and had me, or would have had me
in one more step. But when I heard his breath

hard at my shoulder, I dropped into a ball
and tripped him on the fly. He hit macadam
like a potato sack dropped off a truck
and may have been still skidding by the time
I jumped the Careys' fence and was home safe—
I didn't stay around to pick him up.

His father came that night and wanted Ma
to pay for a doctor and a ruined coat.
But even he, when he saw me, could figure out
Toots had five years, better than twenty pounds,
and at least a foot and a few inches on me.
He had to admit I weighed in as the defender
and that was that. I took my beating later,
when Toots could run again—off to one side:
he'd learned to avoid my wake. And when he caught me,
he only hit for form's sake. Better that
than take a rock in the head when he wasn't looking.

He knew it and I knew it and we were quits.
But I didn't know I knew it till it was done.
And even then I wasn't sure who'd done it
for me or *to* me. Nor even *what* had been done.

The day I broke up Father Ryan's rally
for the Big Green Saint was one more education
in what I hadn't known about myself,
even to guess about, till I lay hiding
among the river cattails, red as murder,
and filling a wax museum with bloody poses
of Trovatore howling down on Carmen
with all blades out and no one giving an inch,
while Rigoletto opened his bloody sack
(that was beside a river, too, I remembered)
and the goddamn Duke, picking up the wrong cue
kept yelling, "*La commedia è finita.*"

I played it out, my belly in a knot
and the weather slanting cold into the night.
I'd gone to communion that morning (I could hear
Sparafucile cackling among the damned
to think what day that was) and had had no breakfast.
I didn't dare go home till after midnight.
And didn't dare go then. And almost didn't,
at least in the role I was half sure I was playing.
For a coat and a sandwich, I'd have hopped a trolley,
stolen a first ride into Sullivan Square,
and jumped whatever was heading into Boston
and out the other side. Or so, at least,
I told myself in whatever part I was playing,
knowing, at curtain time, Ma would be waiting.

Those days she was no one to fool with. Some damn cousin
had worked a sheet of leather into a roll,
bound up one end, and cut the rest to cattails.
Ma kept it for tribal sessions. This would be tribal.
Nor had I ever been closer to the tribe
in my own mood. I knew what was coming next—
I thought I did—and thought I had outgrown it
before it happened. Let her play it hot:
I'd play it cold.   She was sitting in the kitchen
like a stone sybil hissing, the leather cat—
it was my day for cattails—on the table
like a dried familiar, dead but hissing back.
I let her work me over till the welts
bled through my shirt and wouldn't make a sound
except to say, "You having a good time?"
It broke her fit. She was the one to cry.

But everyone played his part in our asylum.
She dropped the cat and stood crying. I picked it up

and tossed it into the garbage. And she kissed me.
And both of us knew it was my confirmation.

—Yes, from *Pagliacci* or from *Rigoletto*.
And yet it was real enough and I was a man,
and frightened her. Had it been Italy,
she thought, she might have watched me climb the mountain
as wronged men go to vengeance where they find it—
wherever the madhouse rocks of history
spin out the numbers of whatever they are
and let a fool and the crumbs of what he has
come through to be taken. She could see me dying
with *carabinieri* smoking out their blood
around the rock I leaped from.
                                    It was that—
guessing what mad histories she read me from—
broke my own madness. How could we ever meet?
I had escaped her, though she washed my back
and oiled it, sobbing her first mood in reverse,
and brought me soup and heated-over spaghetti.
I had escaped her. Would she escape me?
I'd sooner have lost the *Iliad* and the *Odyssey*
than the purity of her madness, which was love
in its own numbered cave. I kissed her forehead
and told her to go to bed and she went to bed,
radiant with my found manhood, as if she dreamed
I had killed the *carabinieri*, gotten away,
gone off to sea and the numbers of destiny
to luck's great seven, and home in a Cadillac
chauffered by a Colonel of *bersaglieri*.
I went to bed myself almost believing
I was a man and had snapped ropes in two,
though I half smelled the grease paint of my fraud.

The skin of my back was pulled too tight for wearing,
but I wasn't about to take off up a mountain
that wasn't there. I had my moods to climb.
And had climbed out of them when I'd played them through
till the next lunacy came from the casting office.

—Meanwhile "At Liberty" as unemployed hams
used to announce in *Variety*. Meaning nowhere,
with nothing to do about it but sit and think.
What had been done? Who did what had been done?
It was so small a step from God that morning.
And took me five more years to finish taking,
sometimes in real sweat, sometimes in real grease paint,
and often enough in both. But I had left
the cave forever, even when I went back
still fingering a guilt like the dry scab
of a cut someone had given me. As I left
that cat-of-twenty-tails in a day's garbage,
curling to question marks on the chicken bones,
as if to ask, "Who chooses what we do?"

I found one part of one answer five years later,
and took thirty more to learn there was not much more.

It was a June day. I was home from school
and curled by my window reading William James
on *The Varieties of Religious Experience*
because a nice-nelly neighbor, half a priest,
and home from the seminary, had sermoned me
when he met me coming from the library
and saw it under my arm. Well, I'd *meant* to read it
or I wouldn't have taken it out, but when he horned in
I decided to take notes to needle him with,
and was working at that. Besides, I was having a fling
at being country gentleman. Come Monday,

I'd have to start another summer's gang
jackhammering for the Gas Co—or for diPietro
who subcontracted for the Gas Co's sweat.
It always took two weeks on the damned hammer
before I could hold my breakfast until lunch,
and at night I'd be hitting my bed, too tired for supper.
Then in ten seconds it would be five o'clock
and time to start again. But this was Thursday
and I was still a scholar.
                              Ma was outside—
my abdicated matriarch and my daughter—
fussing her flowers to bridals by my window.
She was a witch of flowers and could summon them
out of the ground as if they lay full blossomed
and wrapped in mulch, waiting for her to call.
Flowers were her light and gifted as her dark
with tongues she knew, and things did, but no other.
I heard her cooing incantations to them
in the same rhythms I would hear her hiss
when she attacked a dust sent to offend her.
It wasn't enough to scrub it from her floor.
She had to hate it out of the universe.
As she needed now to love her flowers to bloom.
I was taking a killing note on nitrous oxide
("that, by the way," I'd tell him, is laughing gas")
and on what the stuff could do for seminarians
who were running short of mystical experiences,
when I heard a step on the walk, and then the nose
you-know-which Father talked through, asking to know
if I was home.
                    I didn't have to be told
what local priestlet had gone to mass that morning
and stayed to discuss my soul with what local nose.
We all came out being crazy our own way.
But Ma got my soul's medal. "Heesa no home-a,"
I heard her say, defending me on my mountain.

It was as good as any laughing gas
for lifting me to a vision. I saw Time
stripped to Plotinus's and Teresa's bones
and built again to walls and terraces
up the whole mountain I had never seen
out of whose caves my acts came looking for me
like the dark and lighted numbers of a fate
stalked by *carabinieri*, while a sybil,
crouched in a thicket, hissed them to the bone edge
and sent them spinning with a bolt of hate.

—A nose blew through my dream and blew it back,
and Father Ryan was pouring it on Ma
to think of her own soul and of the sin
of letting her son be rotted through by evil
till he was pitchforked screaming into Hell
to wail in the broth forever.
                              Ma didn't exactly
catch all the words but she made out the tune.
If she was my daughter now, she was still a Fury
to any wrong nose that twitched up the mountain.
I heard her scald three thousand guardian years
of a pure mother Arabic, Hebrew, Greek,
Latin, Cave-dialect—you name the tongue
that suffers birth. And if it came out broken
through a slapstick turn of history, it was still
sung from a peak higher than all laughing gases:
"You leava my Johnny alone-a, you Irisha, you.
Heesa goo' boy!"
                 And I was the oaf at the window
when the flowered covenant of language split
to holy truth. I laughed sublimities
and wept whole *fabliaux* for history's daughter
tall from her root of love, my comic source,
my radiant witch of first-made lunacies,

and priestess of the tongues before a man.
"Ma," I whispered, laughing through to prayer,
"I thought you did not know me, nor I you,
but what we are is first milk and last candle,
and indivisibly ahead of thought,
and I am no man till I am your son."

—And closed my great-borne five year step-away
into the first love I identified
my whole way back through time; my first deed done
back to the cave our madness happens from.

The Highest Place in Town

Tufts rises on a drumlin, a pocket of till
fallen from a frayed glacier. Had the ice
sprawled a few miles southeast for the letting go
the Hill might have been an island in Boston Harbor,
had rip tides let it be till piles could shore it
firm to the map.
               Firm to a map old men
kept in their heads to prove a fall from grace,
it made a mile-long sled-run toward the river
till streets and traffic blackened across sled tracks.
Ed Boggs' grandfather swore by cackling Genesis
back to the winter of 1852
when the snow mushed, then froze a two-inch crust,
he'd coasted from the top, across the river,
up the far bank, and on into the swamp.

I listened but didn't believe. The river meadows
ran flat too far once you were off the Hill.
And how had he made it up that mile of slick
to come down longer than history, the old faker?

I squabbled with Ed, claiming it couldn't be done
and ended having to prove it—on a bike
from the top of Winthrop Street, timed to the light
at Boston Ave, with Ed posted halfway
under the trees to signal on the yellow.

I was out of control a hundred yards down, standing
wind-blinded on the brakes, Reos and Fords
honking and climbing the sidewalk out of my slew
till my front wheel broke on a curb and a hedge caught me.

What had I proved of nothing? Ed still believed.
Ma sold the bike to the next junkman by.
The cops took down my name and never forgot.
Months later they hauled me in for wearing bruises
from a fight I hadn't started. The desk sergeant
roared at me down his finger. "There," he said,
"is the freshest kid in Medford!" "Yeah," I told him,
"I work for Al Capone." But when they clanged me
into a cell, I cried—till my sister came
and I had to play tough again. There were no charges:
it was meant to scare me good. But years later,
when I was peddling house-to-house for pennies
I never got, the cops in Arlington
refused me a permit to wear out shoes for nothing
because the son-of-a-bitch that answered the phone
in Medford knew my name.
                              If men were less,
places were more and haunted by long traces.
The Rez was one. The highest place in town.
Some race of giants Grampa Boggs could fable
had terraced another hill above the Hill
and built a crater lake with a brick bottom
lipped by granite slabs and fenced in iron,
with a brick pump house by the college gate.

It formed, I suppose, the hydrostatic head
that firmed our faucets and let fire hoses roar
their rainbows into steam when the red blinked.

82

For me it was the next street to the moon
around those upper acres, an Indian prayer
to blue gods in their valley, King of the Hill
down grass slides steep enough to burn, cops baited
over the fence to run slides on the ice
and away on the other side, nights looking down
for stars in black water, first girls walked
tittering around the sky and down again
with nothing said or seen, boy-packs that sat
waiting for time under the Dipper's arm
and went home without it, aching summer's peak
when the town below gasped sleepless while toy breezes
over the top stirred the hung steams of August.
Time, place, and time-and-place. What names come to
on clear sight lines over the topmost elm
below, ago. Not stopped for and not left.

I almost drowned there once when the ice too late
buckled and gulped a leg; but sprawled flat,
crabbed to the edge on a rubbery inch of water,
ran my wet mile home, and sank into a tub
to shiver back through steam while Ma cried
and slapped me and brought me cocoa and cried again.

In 'thirty-three I used to meet Jim Brown there
to talk books at the stars. In one full moon
we were making up ad-copy based on Veblen
when a football player strolled by, his varsity T
worn on his back and inside out.
                              "By God,"
Jim said, "we make up bad examples, and there goes
the perfect paradigm of Veblen's 'trophy'—
the badge worn with such obvious negligence
that it becomes more obvious."
                              I was sitting

looking away at nothing long down hill.
I had it in mind that Veblen's tribal feathers
were always worn full plumed. But "paradigm"
was a new word to me, and I wanted it
more than another theory. I asked what it meant,
and remember feeling a little disappointed
it hadn't a fancier meaning but liked its sound
and was thinking I could drop it here and there
as a verbal trophy; when I saw a shadow
drop from a tree by the girls' dorm and come past us
and leave its face in the streetlight where Sam Saddle,
who was ten when I was ten, but stayed there,
took home a lank retarded lust whose glands
out-peeped his half mind. Poor man-hulked, boy-dim,
birth-dented skulk of an old hide-and-seek
I left behind a tree where he still played,
but skewed and dangerous in more body than mind.
I watched him lost downhill, off to the night
some cop would tag him out of his own shadow
to cell blocks, while I learned another word.
And sent him, like a prayer, my last learned word:
"God send sweet paradigms of what this is
till the Dipper raise its one hand to a noon
there are no minutes of."

                        "You're muttering,"
Jim said.

              "Sorry. My mind was wandering off
the end of vocabularies."

                    "Maybe a mutter
is the one sound after the last vocabulary."

"Or what vocabularies keep trying to say."

Names. A nameplace. Jim Brown went to work
as an efficiency expert. I went to Bates,
transferred to Tufts, and was back beside the Rez
signed on with the National Youth Administration
to waste time for a federal quarter an hour.
Blue smoky afternoons, the valley's autumn
flaring and rusting north, the iron fence
leaking its shadow to us across the road,
I stood in line with other federalists
on crisps of leaves it was dishonor to rake,
though we had to stir them, and watched Harry Hayford
walk his briefcase like a dog on a choke
to the library and one more inch of note cards
for the term paper I meant to beat him in.
"Go, you sweet bastard, go!" I told a ghost
his shadow left on the leaves, and fell to raking
till the crew hissed and I had to scatter my pile
back on the grass like notes I wasn't taking.

He got his *summa*, damn him, and I missed mine
though I outshouted him whole drunken nights
to prove I had a better thesis going,
or a better bellows for what thesis I had.

Did a little dog's briefcase laugh to see a hill
go over the moon and down again to time?
I had a friend and roared him comedies
as idioms of intention where a stone
dropped by a glacier and gnarled round by roots
is still an echo frozen to a tree.
A namesake locked in place. A word that stays.

It was on the Rez in 1937
I first met Roethke. He and John Holmes, my teacher,
father, friend, and host to my blowfly eggs,

had taught together at Lafayette, and Roethke
was passing through. I was reading on the grass
when John called to me and said the hulk beside him
was Roethke, and told Roethke, stretching a point,
I was a poet.

          I think I said hello
but my throat clicked shut on it. Aside from Holmes
I'd never been near enough to talk to a poet.
And couldn't get near enough then, though there he was.
He asked if I was an athlete. I said No.
He asked my fraternity. I said NYA,
and grinned, and hated myself. There must have been more,
but all I remember from a first of princes
was "No" and one limp quip and—I guess—"Good-bye";
though the next night he looked at some of my poems
and didn't tell me entirely how bad they were.
I was beginning to guess that for myself
but couldn't say it to a prince and a stranger.
I saved it for John Holmes, though not even he
could guess what confessional I'd built around him.

Holmes was key and keyboard. I'd gone to Bates
looking for something and got myself moralized at
and knew that wasn't what I'd been looking for.
I did find Keats—a gift from Roger Fredland—
and heard "the silver snarling trumpets chide,"
"the music yearning like a god in pain."
I was on an aching jag for the free float.
The first poem I turned in for Holmes to praise
(what else do we mean when we ask for criticism?)
was about seeing sharks in Long Island Sound
and being haunted by them—by anything.
"A sense of process, a name of the hunting sea
haunts me," I wrote. Holmes wrote back in the margin:
"All right; you're haunted. When does it haunt me?"

I was never pretty again in any mirror.
I began to learn music comes off the piano
ten-fingered from eighty-eight keys, and that all the god
that yearns in pain speaks that arithmetic
or only burbles. If that seems little to learn,
I haven't finished learning it; nor that love
is the highest place in town, its country spread
to memorize till every name's in place
in its own ghost, returned exact as music.
Time, place, and time-and-place.

                              The Rez came down.
Chain-belt gulpers ate the terraces
down to the roadway. Graders scoured a mall.
Cranes reared and nodded, girders in their jaws.
Bricks climbed the steel. The college crossed the street.

Forty feet down from sky, two arms of dorms
reached down a new field, and Carmichael Hall
crossed them at a perspective's end, not well—
Tufts, alas, is an architectural sin.

Holmes died. I went to Tufts to fill a chair
that took his name. I was housed in a new dorm
just about where I guessed the ice had broken
one day I didn't die, a long cut down
from the shortcut Holmes walked across the sky
home from the college. My first night in that room
I thought I saw the leg I dropped through ice
still dangling from the ceiling. John Holmes strolled
over my head looking at everything
in another world.
                    I went to Carmichael Lounge
to talk to students, a fumble of good intentions.
My first day there a fat boy asked a question

that still droops like a dead flag into weathers
nothing can breathe. "How does it feel," he said,
"to be a success?"
                I sat a dead man's chair
trying to name mortality to an oaf
too pink-eared to begin. What bones lay buried
that hill down from a sky-top lost! Moon over
a January wood ticking with cold
and round an iron fence with stars boxed in it
Whiteside came at me. How could I have guessed
he meant to marry her?—that bed was mine.
And still he came on round a fence of stars
like a sign from a warped zodiac: *Sponsus* flaming,
the Bridegroom in ascendance, *Virgo* fallen,
Amicus in eclipse under the wheel
that turns men queer and sad and caught between
loves and ironies, mad as the stars once beat
another kind of reason for what we are,
yet feeling what we feel as if it were real.

I had a friend and froze to a dumb question.
My toes were ice cubes. Membranes in my nose
glazed sharp when I breathed in. What comedy
was turning numb and sad? A lie could turn it.
Could I turn from the lie and not be damned?

I heard him quoting from a horoscope:
"You owe me the truth."
                       "I owe you something better."
"I'll settle for that."
                I heard an idiot tell him,
and nothing moved.
                "You wanted the truth," I said.
"That's half of it. If you want the other half,
I'm sorry but not guilty. I mean sorry

for as good a reason as yours."
                              "I know," he said,
but nothing moved.
                              I thunked my mile down hill
like January wood. The wind behind me
rattled the dead hedge that had caught me once
on the way to proving nothing. "Thanks," I told it,
and made it home again, almost in reason,
if there was reason and we were parts of it.

We never again were friends. A hill came down.
Somebody died. An idiot asked a question
of the idiot who gave answers. A name went out
like candelabra blown to smoky letters.
John Holmes came ambling home over the sky hump
counting miles out from the wind in no hurry,
looking at everything in his own time.

"Evening, Inspector Holmes. What's that out there?"
"A world, sir. Mine."
                              "Inspector, what is a world?"

"A world—as even you might see by looking—
is three steps out to God: first green, then blue,
then purple."
                    "Then God, Inspector?"
                                            "And then God."
"In any direction?"
                    "Just one: out from the center."
"Out—there?"
                    "Out there as well as any."

"Well now, Inspector, you'll note I pointed to Stoneham.
Are you ready to claim for the Unitarian *logos*
Stoneham is the last purple step to God?
—Remember purple turns to green when you get there."

"And green to blue again, and blue to purple,
and still three steps to God."
                              "Inspector Holmes,
why does the question change from where it is
to wherever you happen to be, once you have gone there?"

"That, sir, is called the mystery."
                              "It sounds shifty.
But as long as God stays Unitarian
the question's academic. Which allows me
to get back to the center, which is: how are you?
what sort of day have you had?"
                              "A good three-stepper
at an altitude above you mundane types.
Come over later: a batch of new books came."

And went home then. Calling a name and no answer.
A habit that had been love. Well then, a drink.
Whatever is after nothing. Hell, take the bottle
and up to the study a while . . .
                              and the woman there.
Red-handed. Wrists slashed. And what she had swallowed.
All propped in a chair in the middle of the room,
three walls of books torn down to rubble round her.
An anatomy of motives stated: *Over
my dead body.* Said in that one room,
the one he closed the door to, never again
alone there. A suicide not good-bye
but a staying change. *Whenever you come again
I will say this to you again who am here forever,
married closer than love, the door flung wide.
And what will you see when you dare look?*

                              Ah, John,
what faces faces change to down from love,

the highest place come down: a fat oaf there
fumbling sincerities that only smudge
the three-colored country out to mist!
You should have been a Wordsworth of unevent
in a little country of kindness, real or not,
but changing only from green to blue to purple
to the last mist that changes when we near,
success forgiven, every failure love
that cannot fail what it forgives, that dies
finding the name that says us, real or not,
still sounding at the center of the mist
that thinks itself: time, place, and time-and-place.

Ghosts a ghost lives by. Gone from but not left.

The Graph

By time and after, where the guessed-at dead
curled in, unborn, and charred before they hit,
or blew to gases when their tanks cooked off,
or only passed forever through one cloud;
we manned wired systems, and the diagrams
wavered on blue mirages like decals
washed off a sunken panel, whole but warped.

What do the dying die to? Lost names plunged
a graph of smoke like a Black Friday crash,
and told names flipped a toggle's bombs away.
Pig-iron carcasses followed falling. Hammers
an atmosphere away beyond dogged hatches
banged on the pressured roof. A slant of comets
fell off the long sky home. Peeled sores of towns
stained photos magnified to the misty grain
then focused back to what detail showed through
—never the dead—to paper orderlies
who plotted, dot by dot, a guessed-at graph:
MAN HOURS OF PRODUCTION INTERDICTED.
(Generals are phrased by clerks.) And month on month
we hit more shacks and paddies than factories.
The graph wormed nowhere at the foot of the cliff
the dead scrawled down the statistician's eye.

Is dying anything? We buried names.
A clerk with a wet rag was priest enough
for last rites at the crewboards. Each wiped name
proved us our own, one number nearer home,
and never near enough. Our own lies dreamed us.
I practiced thinking I had died last week
and could relax with nothing more to lose.
Still in the night sweat before every mission
a wet rag whispered: "By this time tomorrow
you may have burned to death." My kept name cried
over a surf-soughed sea-cliff to Orion
sinking to tops of salted scrub-pine shadow:
"Then what do I want tonight, if I could have it?"
And having scoured from galaxies to the cellar
of the last bone, it found man's three last wishes
just as the wiped names left them in their dream:
"A woman, whiskey, and a T-bone, rare."

I didn't die, nor did I get my wishes
this side of life again and a sea across,
though every landing back from fantasy
I got two shots of the Flight Surgeon's rye
(Imagine dying on anything less than bourbon!)
and told my tale, the nothing I could tell
of the last sighted names, of slanting comets,
of kills and probables and bombs away,
and diagrams that rippled off still whole.

We went neat courses to graph-numbered reasons:
what Mitsubishi's lathes could not turn out,
no gun could fire; what his assembly lines
could not assemble, never would take off.

But though we put our cross hairs on his roofs,
wind frayed the bombing tables. The jet stream raged

past our last given numbers. The dead went down
steeper than bombs to nothing. Three months' dying
the stalled graph stuck.
                    Then a two-star LeMay,
(later he went to four and then to clinkers)
a wet cigar butt in his carcass jaw,
took over the graph: machines we couldn't hit
were run by men, and men who sleep in houses
can be burned out. We went in low at night
loaded with firesticks we spewed out like nails
from busted kegs, and, with an edge of wind,
scabbed fifty-two square miles of Tokyo.

The graph took off for heavens of fantasy
slide rules compound like prayer wheels. God shall learn
His last from statisticians. One of ours
had beeped back home for fire-insurance tables
of prewar Tokyo, drawn an overlay,
and marked our drop-points where the rates were highest.

His numbers and two stars in God's own wind
set off a firestorm in the tinder flats.
A clerk cartoonist drew flames on the graph
where it charred up the numbers. (Generals
are taught to laugh by clerks.) But all I saw
looked like a city dump burning at night
below a bluff.
                    Somewhere inside the mist
of the last grain at its last magnification
rats of our hot statistics sniffed a panic,
dancing their circles on the shrinking darks
to writhe there twitching when the air gave out
inside the firewall cones like little Fujis
spewing an emperor's holiday of sparks,
until the sucked-out air sucked in the firewalls
to gasp up blowtorch flues burned in the sky.

—I guessed this much by linking fossil facts.
What I saw sank to nothing much behind us:
sparks of a burned-out graph, its dots and dashes
disjointed, never visible, and not ours.
So, death surmised from bone—as anthropologists
guess out a face for the Neanderthal.

The one death I will swear I knew the face of
that dying year—knew it as if I were
its own ghost to the end—was F.X.Mannion's,
Foxy Mannion, our altar-boy navigator
who prayed his odds like Stations of the Cross,
a rosary to the number, his map-table
so Christopher'd and Virgin'd and be-Jesus'd
he had to hold his pencil in his teeth
or never draw a course this side of Heaven.

God keep clear Angels plotted to His stars
and draw man's line straight on the Rose of Winds
across blank parallels and meridians,
and call him out and back, and let no blast
deflect his courses, and let F.X.Mannion
be suffered whole where certainties are solved.

I send this prayer to faiths I do not need
for the boy Mannion, saint of his own terrors,
who never linked two words wholly his own
but blurred a quivering *Credo* at every flak burst,
a *Paternoster* at every Zero sighted,
and, when the hammers pounded on the roof,
fisted a scapular and unreeled to God
at a thousand mumbo-jumbo r.p.m.'s
whole litanies recorded at slow rote
where adolescents at the sulphur-stinking
guilt edge of flesh fall to their lonely sin
in God's eye and the terrors they are taught.

Still, more or less, by our asylum rules
he passed for normal—meaning he'd made it back
as often as he'd left—till the payday night
he broke the crap game at the Officers Club.
He had twelve thousand in the Day Room safe,
all labeled and rubber-banded and receipted,
when he woke up next morning sweating terror.
He'd had a dream that luck is a fixed ration.
An Angel or his Virgin Mother had warned him:
luck used up on dice comes off the odds
that keep men on the roster. When night came
he drew his cash for the high-roller wipe-out
against the first-night kings from all four Groups.
He went for broke on every long-side odds.
He rolled and let it ride pass after pass.
When the game broke, he had to take his shirt off
and wrap the greenbacks in it like dirty laundry.
And when he woke, his next green morning sweat,
his new receipt read forty-seven thousand.

"My God," he told me, sweating, "I tried to *lose!*"
—He lied, of course. No one *can't* lose at craps.
But he was young and greedy and drunk on luck
he'd never known and had to take as guilt.

He was up for that night's mission. God only knows
what r.p.m.'s of litany he spun
over the line he reeled in from the stars
and inched on his mercator to Nagoya.
It broke off there. And if death's guessable,
I'll stake my own—take all or any part—
I heard his final record spun so fast
its grooves outflamed the firewash he dove spieling:
O Holy Mary, Mother of God, I knew it!
O-Holy-Mary-Mother-of-God-I-knew-it!

oholymarymotherofgodiknewit!
—beeping through circuit hum and the squeal of space.

Message received: guilt makes the dark that comes
out of all averages. If men can bear
the mathematics of which they are the chances,
nameless as particles, this was a boy
in the boy rites of war, and he died rich
of all he could not spend of his own guilt.

And if I raid him for a foolish fact,
he did not need his own death, and I do.
For though I studied dying all that year,
saying its names to memory and the moon,
the only dead I saw were souvenirs
from a marine's grimoire, or a saint's dreambook,
or Hieronymus Bosch drunk in the devil's tank,
where corpses shed their living tongues to dark.

I have their telling from the globing moon.
The Quonset snored and sweated. Half down a bottle,
I took a blanket, flashlight, cigarettes,
and filled my canteen at the Shinto Shrine,
half-seas over in the full moon spill.
Two walls and a chow-lion glowed from shadow
as hands and numbers float a wristwatch dial.
The ground crews' tents were pyramids on sticks,
or geometric icebergs in a searchlight:
two facets glaring and two darks asleep.

Drink to what glares from dark. Rays like pale slats
crisscross and cannot hold it. It walks on drums.
The whistle of its whim through decoy angels
blasts hot dawns from their silos. Stickmen dance
through aureoles under it. And at the treetops

black Boanergeses gun it. Their red spit whinnies
across the coral, powdering drifts of ghosts.

Drink to it—to anything. Rye sinks in its bottle.
A drunk sprawls on a beach under a sea-cliff
white as the skull of Argos, socketed
with all the hundred burned caves of his eyes.
I see the moon: a lit tank of sauterne
that stays filled as it spills, the wine aglow
through all the hunch of sea past a black headland.
What cannot find us in the dark of heaven
will have its ray tonight. I see the island
black-etched and sea-lace-trimmed on the lit spill,
home-clear in the hunter's eye. Drink to the hunter.
Four fingers from the bottom the wailers wind
a cyclone up the sky and itchy fingers
poke flak holes high in nothing. I pick a cave,
bottle in one hand, flashlight in the other
—and there were all the dead I ever saw
that dying year, where the flamethrowers had left them
blown back to the inner wall and toppled over
on one another, sizzled to dry to rot,
or so I guessed (and maybe sea-air salted).
Which pocket of Hell was that? Drink to them all.

A tourist there before me had left a keg.
A minute in Hell and all arrival's over.
Sledges, miles off, thumped rock. Spent flak
pattered white dust-ghosts from the ledge. I sat
(two minutes in Hell and any man is home
with nothing else to do) and played my beam
over the damned, and all were duplicates:
heads back as if from broken necks, mouths gaping
wider than they had faces for. A cord

of stacked saints waiting for their horn, or hellkins
discharged from God's will to wait back to dust.

Drink to Malebolge! "Hey, Brother Francis,"
Four Roses called through Hell, "You there, corpse lover,
scraping your flesh to God and the biota
between love's hair shirt and Old Body Grease—
we're down to what comes after all kissed sores.
Which of these would you be, old amateur,
could you have your God-druthers?—this one?"
I beamed him a ray to choose by. "Like this one better?"
I lit another gasper and heard the thudding
change to trip-hammers. "No, no. Two knocks for yes.
One knock for no. Don't mumble." The thudding slackened.
"That's better: space your answers.—How about this one?"
I lit another and heard *thud-thud-thud.*
"No triple thumping," I warned. But still no answer.
"You there—Hieronymus Bosch. Yes, you on the left—
you think I wouldn't know your face in Hell?—
which one of these is Francis at his dream's end?
This one, you say?" I sucked the bottle dry,
beamed in on a gape that had no bottom to it,
and heard the bottle drop, bounce, and not break,
sucking the whiskey out of me into dark:

inside the mouth hole of the gaping mummy
a light-tipped tongue wagged chittering!
                              Then the rat
leaped out and blurred away across the dark
faster than I could follow with my light.

A half hour into Hell and most is known.
Two other tongues wagged and went skittering
before the raid thumped out, the All Clear sounded,

and I went sober Sunday'd to the moon
preaching what saints are made of, who can't rot
but only wait God's leaping word out; preaching
all Hell's a sot's rave till, the All Clear sounding,
it's a rat heaven, each in his lived-in feast,
his meat mine of safe blisses to eat out
till light shines through the skin of what we are,
and dotted boys and signing generals,
and moonbone saints aglow above a dark,
all wag a heaven tongue that none can speak
till all do, and in idiom.

               I climbed back
and lived, my numbers changing their years out
to guessed-at dots of what there is to graph;
and write what I remember of the dead,
our duplicates and their own in the globing moon.

Two Saints

White toga'd God of the gold sandals
that do not touch; Grandfather Mercy
to good boys in their lantern of prayer;
to the evil in me, Thunder—oh Whirlpool Eye
whose mote I was down lenses and spiral tubes
where spun light came apart and I fell through
to the terrible otherness I must become
who could not become myself—this last time down
the lens turned backwards to queer dwindling points
I exorcise the terrors I died small of
there in my midge-days' madness.
                                   Small?
The size there was. Your spider was dream enough;
its web, a continent. You, First Father Guilt
forever cocked at the center, my sleep tossed
on the threads of your least stirring.
                                   My made guilt
made me food. And then idea. Idea, Father,
is to grapple, not forgive. And what had I
to wrestle thought to, blackfriar'd as I came
past pitch and rumor? Your black priests lessoned me:
good served no good without their laying on:
St. Joe's was the one door and Hell the parish
of every other: though they were friends and kind,
no prayer could save them. But could I have a friend

and say yes to his damnation? deny a friend
and not be damned?
                   When Willie Crosby drowned,
I followed in my tears to a wrong church
I dared not enter, knowing the ground would open
to gulp me burning, or lightning cinder me.
I could not kneel by my friend. He was wet forever,
the light slammed in his eyes, his hair flowing
in tanks of Hell—who had done no wrong, and had lent me
a dime I could never repay but gave for him
to Ralph, the beggar, who sat his legless wait
on a four-wheeled shelf by Woolworth's, offering pencils
it would be death to take.
                      Were his legs buried?
Would he be ghosted to them in fathering time
and walk where Willie swam after all chances?
Is accident a thing?
                "God wanted Willie,"
the priest told me.
                And chose *that* way to call him?
Knowing he wasn't even a Catholic?
A boy to murder and then send to Hell?

"All things are in His will."
                  He *meant* it?
—I saw the cramp like an aimed shark in clear water.
I saw God squeeze my friend into a fist,
then drop him blue-pale in a sleep of weeds
till the black grapple stirred him, not awake.

. . . And if there is no accident? Oh spheres
crystals and bells and spires of a planned light
I tried to see by, the meridian blaze
that hurls the godless dark, not of Its will
but theirs, the dark within them

102

returning of itself to its own nature,
all purposed, all purposeful. . . . No, I could not believe.
If all was God then half of God was evil.

"Ah, blasphemy! Will you dare ask God His reasons?"
said the shadow in the confessional.
                                        Could I dare
ask less of anything? I was half damned,
but could not give Willie up.
                                        And then forgot him.
Forgot the tears of my first heresy.
I stood alone at the stone-shadowed door
of a wrong church and watched a box go in,
the door swing shut its oak-carved cross on traffic.
A crack ran through the right arm of the cross
and still the cross stayed whole. Seemed to stay whole.
I saw the crack reach gaping through the world
and Willie falling in to a root tangle.
And left before the door opened again.

And then forgot. I had my dog to love,
a year to turn. A madness like a nature
closed seamless as water over a day's drowning.
My legs were animals with themselves to run.
I could not die forever in a thought.

But I had thought a dying up to God
in His confessional, and what was whispered
had been no father to me, though I prayed
as I was whispered. Why did He send me thoughts
that turned to sins? I had not asked to think.
If doubts came, were they mine? I prayed for lilies
out of His garden and was sent a thicket.
If what He sent was sin, whose was the sin?

And still my legs were their own animals
and ran me into light where I forgot,
being glad of energy and half self-solved:
if evil was His sending, how could I
be other than He made me, safe and free
from the boy killed to show me what He meant?

"Of the objectivity of self," said Kiro
a whiskey time later, "take the Siberian sparrow
that lit on a fresh cow flop in February
and there sang spring songs till it froze to the turd.
If man's no bird, he'll take what heat he finds.
I'll be your dollop of truth: nest in the thought,
you shivering fluff: it steams the better for stinking:
man's what sings his accidents to conclusion."

"No," I said, "to conclusions."
                                    "That's just to say
there are many plops in the pasture. There's just one
      weather.
And only the same bird always from like eggs.
Take your own case, you lost Dominican
drizzle of second reasons: had your father died
when you were seven and wanting your mother back,
you'd have been guilty of having wished him dead.
When he happened to die, you would have been his killer.
I'll bet a beatification or thirty-two cents—
whichever you think you can deliver first—
you'd be in skirts today, beating your chest
to be sure God had an earful of your guilt,
and preaching others guilty—that's accidence.

"But come to the altar purified for praise,
you'd sing off-key. And back in your saint's cell
there'd be cobwebs on your prayer book, but manuscripts

of notes on canon law. *That* is conclusion:
wherever accidence takes you, it's your conclusion
to sing off-key and nit-pick among loopholes.

"As it happened—accidence—the old man kicked off
while you were still all sour milk and sweet love,
and all the guilt you ever felt was taught you
like another language you never could pronounce,
you lucky bastard. And still, you self-concluded
word-dizzy shyster, you swindle among footnotes,
and can't sing Cause on key. Since God hasn't,
I damn you personally. Now have a drink."

I had the drink. Ah, Kiro, could I pour
a sweeter rhetoric than any I heard
from God's anointed mouths, I'd make a psalm
of the dancer in his arc, of a style of time
to an Okinawan cross; of man, the monstrance
of a pig-iron fragment that might as well
have cut a leaf from a tree; of my friend, the dancer,
dead in the epilogue of an island war
in which no shore was home, nor the sea, place.

A man's what recognizes accident
as the environment. Born of his chances,
dead of the last, his interim is style,
which is to say, his way of choosing reactions
to chances that do not kill, his contract made
with killing chances—a principle of selection
selecting itself.

                    Kiro, I need to say this,
no longer to you. A saint with a sense of humor
might carve dice from his bones and pray with those.
If his mind was easy—as no saint's is entirely

105

in the idiom of God—he'd spare himself
by borrowing used bones and rolling those.
Why amputate for nothing? The point is not
to see how much can be lopped and the man live,
but to note the numbers turning into fact.

Kiro, you damned me once and in good whiskey.
Would you again, if out of another bottle
I take you for that easier saint, not saved
but selfless?—in ego, a companion of egoes:
not ego itself, but ego recognized
as an animal attachment, an organ of guess,
the failure that forgives by its own flaws
recognized in another? And then danced to
because the man's a dancer in his own conclusion
after all accidence— If that's half a creed,
its graces are fact, scope, and irony.

"Feet, soap, and idiocy," I heard his ghost
chuckle inside my head. "One blind boy saint
to crack a hole in the dark. And now a blind man
to lead you to the light. That's hagiography?
You're still a swindler, bless you—or be damned:
whichever it is you always really wanted.
I never knew which for sure, nor ever can now."

"I wanted to be sane. Saner at least
than what I'd come from. And I wanted to love.
Want to. And can. And do. You, among others."

"Then drink up. Thirst's a blessing. And when the bottle
smashes on the last number, that's not damnation,
but no mouth, and no saying, and no thirst
—till some damned fool a shadow might have loved
tries stirring up the shadow that isn't there."

I forget what Willie looked like. I see his bottom
shinnying trees above me, hands packing snowballs,
my liver-colored dog that ran between us,
a bubble up from weeds. And that door shut
on a church that could poison me like the black idea
of a drowned boy wasted inside its wrongness,
yet something like a saint, having gone so far.

And because his dying changed my first of reasons.

As Kiro changed to words in a bad letter.
"Hey, by the way, you remember Kiroiates—
weren't you two sort of chummy?—the poor bastard
got it on Okinawa. Grenade fragment.
I hear he's up for maybe a pretty good medal—
if you happen to have a taste for the posthumous.
He always was a classy son-of-a-bitch.
I wish I'd known him better. Well, so it goes.
Don't you go bucking for ribbons. This war's over
with only some strictly surplus dying left."

Do I remember him chuckling in my head?
—"I've seen worse epitaphs and heard worse advice.
Anything's better than what governments write
and G.I. crosses. Imagine *me* under a cross.
The goddamn least a grateful country could do
for its more articulate drunks, dead in Supply,
is to leave a space on dog tags that codes out:
'Religion: bourbon. Marker: broken bottle.' "

. . . Yet something like a saint, having come so far
to change me to a good I had once prayed for
and never reached but by the revelation
a man is in the dauntlessness of style.
The kindness of defeat that quips to graces.

To a dead boy and a dead man in my head
I loved and half forgot, loved and remembered.

I doubt there is much more to what we are.

Epilogue: The Burial of the Last Elder

He died in unknown tongues. Latin he'd heard
the lifelong Sunday cant and cadence of
but not the words, came, mispronounced, to pray him
between a brogue and its South Boston slur,
but right enough, being as far as God.
English he hadn't learned in seventy years
walked round his name. He was the last where none
could sing the yokel cadence of his mountain—
not dialect but defeat, a tribe's long waste
from father stones it could no longer read;
and still a man's first-said good morning home
where light's the mother-door, where all deaths go
their last breath back, what no man leaves for long.

He'd never left but only stretched a visit
into a way of life on a tourist visa
that never quite expired—until he heard
a cock crow and his dog bark and remembered
they were dead in another country a world ago;
but idioms yet a while, as all tongues are
spoken by memory to a habit of hearing.

An idiom closed. That night above New York,
stacked up above a fog, I found Arcturus
off the Big Dipper's handle, then faded down
from galaxies to mist and landed nowhere

down sight lines of blind instruments, and so home—
wherever that is that the dead ignore.

I buried mine and took my own away.
Sweet mornings to the mountain that begins.
Good dancing and good wine, its feast day come.
Goodnight to sons gone down a sea away
and washed back to the stones of a first name.
He lived where nothing meant but only stood
between him and returning, and had forgotten
how to return except as bones must stir
a dust made for them they themselves will make
till names come off the land, and then, and after.

And had forgotten he had never left.

I took my own away. What shall I hear
my last hark back to time? Not where I live.
Nowhere I happen to be. Not where I was.
I never lived anywhere but by accident,
and never went anywhere I meant to stay
till I found I owned a house and lived in it
between jets anywhere. And never knew
my neighbor on either side until the day
my garage roof burned. And never saw either again,
though sometimes a horn honks and an arm waves
and I wave back, not quite sure what I mean,
not sure to whom I mean it.

                                    I keep an idiom,
and stay another day and then another,
stretching a tourist visa past the stones
that settle into habits, landmarks noted,
the little place just off the avenue
where someone was young once, and the young still go

in their other idiom, though the easy streets
a walk-up to a love-ago are dangerous
in sentiment and fact, now animal shadows
crouch, hooked to habits they must kill to keep,
tourists of their own means to heaven a while.

I have nowhere to come from or return to,
or when I do go back, it isn't there.
The house is paid for and that's home enough.
Resident persuaders in panel trucks
roar from bullhorns, swearing me to live here.

What could I tell my dead of what I do?

Last month I caught a cab in Philadelphia
bound for Penn Station. A bullhorn roared for Nixon.
The street jammed shut. I paid the cabby off
and wedged my way afoot to catch a train
to where I could vote No. I jumped it
its first wheel round, slid into a seat, slid back
eleven years: I was walking my wife through Rome
the night a salmon-run came lunging
up electronic falls to Piazza Venezia,
and fishermen came howling from every bank,
dove into the boil, and lunged there with the salmon
up a cascade of blather. I remembered
Quasímodo droning lipless through the mask
a Sicilian mother-sybil left him: "The Greeks
invented civil war. The Italians, alas,
perfected it." There up the amplified falls
perfected art roared in the rage of Cause.

"Good Lord, what's that?" my wife said.
                                    The falls bellowed:
GIUSTIZIA (*screeeeeee*) IL POPOLO (*scru—ooo**k***).

AGGIORNAMENTO (*iiiiiigh*) ITALIA (*glooorp*)
"Artifacts of perfected art," I told her.
"What?" she cried in the roar. "What did you say?"
"Visible mercy: a war I don't have to go to."
"WHAT?"
              "POLITICS. ABSOLUTION POLITICS."
Around the corner: "Did you say absolution?"
"Yes. Mine. From slogans I don't have to shout."

But could I have told my dead in Heaven or Hell
what I was doing in 1948
six cascade nights a week for Henry Wallace
in the perfected barreling of a cause
I couldn't myself believe but by outshouting
the calms of mind names come to when they come,
closer than salmon run their falling water?

Two months and a week or two before November,
having been granted an evening with The Man
as my reward for frenzy, I lay awake
knowing the man was wrong, the Cause sold,
and that my calendar was signed and sworn to
for another sixty nights in the cascades
I was the bullhorn of . . . and lunged my way
toward nothing, up Columbias I was trapped in
till—the confessional and November come,
the curtain closed behind me—I made my cross
for Truman, and went home from Cause forever,
in idiom with the dead, whose shrug forgives
wrong sons the imperfect art of being men.

I was still walking backwards from absolution
a first block up the Corso, when my window
flashed neon: TRENTON MAKES—THE WORLD TAKES.

What made me think of Perry in '44,
my bearded con-man beach-rat buddy stripped
to shorts and GI boots and a tan so native
he could have passed for the dawn age in decay?
Outside our mess hall three black boiling troughs
steamed absolution—soap, disinfectant, rinse—
and the loin-clothed rabble stank by in the roar
of sanitation to dip its mess kits pure,
cautious as sinners in their bowing hour
before the power locked in the sacrament.
Till a replacement in full uniform
and even creases, slammed his kit in the boil,
spraying a scald, and Perry jumped back yelling:
CHRISSAKE WATCH WHATCHA DOING! THAT'S
   HOTCHA MEATHEAD!

The oaf glared at the bum: WHYNCHA WEAR PANTS?
And Perry, from the throne of his contempt
for fools still dressed for Sunday School in Hell:
PANTS ARE NO PROTECTION AGAINST IGNORANCE.

DUTCH BOY, the window said. COVERS THE WORLD.

SHE MAY LOOK INNOCENT, said a latrine poster,
BUT PROTECT YOUR PANTS.
                        And then the window again:
HAD YOU BUILT IN BRUNSWICK YOU WOULD BE HOME NOW.

. . . Over the waterfall roaring of the wheels,
slogan by slogan to a town called home. . . .

At Stelton I thought of a traveler from Thackeray's Brussels
(not Smedley—he had bought his horses and fled)
climbing a church tower out of cannon range
of Waterloo, and watching through a glass

deaths so small their uniforms stayed neat
though whole men were ripped out of them.
                              May I learn
a mercy beyond recruitment. I have folded
my last dead to their names and have no father.
Let what I love outlive me and all's well.
Bless everyman his wandering never home.
Bless him his dead and fold them to a name
he can pronounce his last breath back, and keep him
the tourist of his means, toward heaven a while.

I have no worlds to change and none to keep.

Lives of X

Talking Myself to Sleep
at One More Hilton

I have a country but no town.
Home ran away from me. My trees
ripped up their white roots and lay down.
Bulldozers cut my lawn. All these
are data toward some sentiment
like money: God knows where it went.

There was a house as sure as time.
Sure as my father's name and grave.
Sure as trees for me to climb.
Sure as behave and misbehave.
Sure as lamb stew. Sure as sin.
As warts. As games. As a scraped shin.

There was a house, a chicken run,
a garden, guilt, a rocking chair.
I had six dogs and every one
was killed in traffic. I knew where
their bones were once. Now I'm not sure.
Roses used them for manure.

There was a house early and late.
One day there came an overpass.
It snatched the stew right off my plate.
It snatched the plate. A whiff of gas
blew up the house like a freak wind.
I wonder if I really mind.

My father died. My father's house
fell out of any real estate.
My dogs lie buried where time was
when time still flowed, where now a slate
stopped river loops, called Exit Nine.
Why should I mind? It isn't mine.

I have the way I think I live.
The doors of my expense account
open like arms when I arrive.
There is no cloud I cannot mount
and sip good bourbon as I ride.
My father's house is Hilton-wide.

What are old dog bones? Were my trees
still standing would I really care?
What's the right name for this disease
of wishing they might still be there
if I went back, though I will not
and never meant to?—Smash the pot,

knock in the windows, blow the doors.
I am not and mean not to be
what I was once. I have two shores
five hours apart, soon to be three.
And home is anywhere between.
Sure as the airport limousine,

sure as credit, sure as a drink,
as the best steak you ever had,
as thinking—when there's time to think—
it's good enough. At least not bad.
Better than dog bones and lamb stew.
It does. Or it will have to do.

The text of this book was set in Linotype Century Schoolbook and printed by offset on P & S Special Book manufactured by P. H. Glatfelter Co., Spring Grove, Pa. Composed by Cherry Hill Composition, Pennsauken, N.J. Printed and bound by Quinn & Boden Company, Inc., Rahway, N.J.